"This book is excellent and would be helpful to a lot of people who are keen to engage with Tibetan Buddhism seriously as a practice and a way of being in the world."

THUPTEN JINPA LANGRI, PhD, Religious Studies; English Translator for His Holiness the Dalai Lama XIV

"She writes as a Westerner who has found inner freedom through the very same teachings and practices that help to keep such a beautiful smile on His Holiness's face . . . in spite of all of life's challenges. Your understanding of our human predicament, and the path to lasting happiness, will be richly enhanced by reading this lovely book."

JOHN E. WELSHONS, author of *One Soul, One Love, One Heart* and *Awakening from Grief*

"With Lama Tsomo's quick, sometimes edgy humor, and a good dose of her sweet grace, and genuine empathy, the learning process is really very joyous!"

ALLISON TROXEL, artist and student of Lama Tsomo

"Lama Tsomo teaches with an open, nonjudging heart. Her personal stories, her humor, her well-chosen metaphors gently welcome those new to Buddhist insights. Whether you are 'just' curious about how the threatened, exiled Dalai Lama can live in joy . . . or you feel ready to apply the book's careful, specific instruction in your own life, this book is perfect."

FRANCES MOORE LAPPÉ, author of *Diet for a Small Planet* and *EcoMind*

"Designed for readers from all backgrounds and levels of experience, this beautiful book offers step-by-step guidance in accessible practices, as well as a rich array of stories, scientific perspectives and ways of dealing with challenges that arise on the path. You will find in these pages a precious invitation to inhabit the happiness, love and freedom of your own awakened heart."

TARA BRACH, PhD, author of *Radical Acceptance* and *True Refuge*

"This highly readable, extraordinarily informative and practical guide by Lama Tsomo, an American female lama, is sprinkled with detailed and specific instructions in Tibetan Buddhist meditation practices and with concrete suggestions for promoting happiness and well-being."

RICHARD J. DAVIDSON, Founder, Center for Healthy Minds, University of Wisconsin—Madison

"Before Lama Tsomo, I felt meditation was only in the mind. Through these practices, I felt it come into my heart. Through Lama Tsomo, I found more freedom, laughter and grace. I honor her as a teacher and am grateful she has brought these ideas into a format that is accessible to more people."

MARIANNE MANILOV, student of Lama Tsomo; founder, Engage Network

TIBETAN BUDDHIST PRACTICE SERIES

Ancient Wisdom for Our Times

BOOK 2 *Wisdom & Compassion*

(Starting with Yourself)

TIBETAN BUDDHIST PRACTICE SERIES

Ancient Wisdom
for Our Times

BOOK 2 *Wisdom & Compassion*
(Starting with Yourself)

Lama Tsomo

foreword by HIS HOLINESS THE DALAI LAMA XIV

Namchak

Namchak

PUBLISHING

Namchak

PUBLISHING

The Namchak Foundation supports the study and practice of the Namchak Lineage of Tibetan Buddhism.

Namchak.org

Cover design: Kate Basart/Union Pageworks
Book design: Mary Ann Casler & Kate Basart/Union Pageworks
Cover art from *The Encyclopedia of Tibetan Symbols and Motifs* by Robert Beer, © 1999 by Robert Beer. Reprinted by arrangement with Shambhala Publications, Inc., Boulder, CO. www.shambhala.com.
Editorial: Michael Frisbie
Copyeditor: Erin Cusick/Cusick Editing
Indexer: Michael Ferreira/Ferreira Indexing, Inc.
Project and print management: Elizabeth Cromwell/Books in Flight
Printed in Canada

Printed on FSC-certified materials with vegetable-based ink

FSC
www.fsc.org

MIX
Paper from responsible sources
FSC® C016245

Library of Congress Control Number: 2021908700

ISBN: 978-1-951096-90-8

First printing, 2021

26 25 24 23 22 21   1 2 3 4 5 6 7 8

Contents

Tulku Sangak Rinpoche

Homage

In the Tibetan tradition, I want to begin by paying homage to my Root Lama, Gochen Tulku Sangak* Rinpoche, who has guided me with patience, wisdom, and a good helping of humor, since the beginning of my pursuit of the Vajrayana path. Studying at his feet has been like standing with my mouth open, under a waterfall. As with glaciers flowing to waterfalls, truth and inspiration flow in abundance from the Buddha, through the masters of this lineage, and through Rinpoche. I continue to receive this gift in wonder and gratitude.

---

* Sometimes spelled *Sang-ngag*.

"When the iron bird flies and horses run on wheels, the Tibetan people will be scattered like ants across the face of the world, and the Dharma will come to the land of red faces."

—*Prediction by Guru Rinpoche, the enlightened Indian master who caused Buddhism to take root in Tibet in the ninth century* CE

Tulku Sangak Rinpoche, His Holiness the Dalai Lama XIV, *Lama Tsomo*

THE DALAI LAMA

FOREWORD

As our world becomes ever more connected, the world's great spiritual traditions are able to get to know each other better. This provides their followers opportunities to learn from one another and develop a deeper appreciation and respect for each other's teachings, traditions and practices. I, for one, have learned a great deal from the insights of spiritual traditions other than my own.

I often describe myself as a staunch Buddhist. However, I have never felt the urge to propagate Buddhism with the aim of converting others to my point of view. In general, I believe it's better and safer for most people to stay within the religious tradition of their birth. The world's faiths evolved in specific geographical and cultural circumstances, which gives them an affinity to the spiritual inclinations and needs of specific communities. I am quite open about this, especially when I am asked to speak about Buddhism in the West, where the main spiritual traditions are historically Judeo-Christian.

At the same time, I recognize that, especially in today's interconnected world, there will be individuals who find the approach of traditions other than those to which they were born to be more effective and suited to their own spiritual aspirations. I know many people in the West, in both North America and Europe, who engage in serious study and practice of Buddhist teachings. They find the advice for training the mind presented in the Buddhist teachings to be profoundly beneficial and meaningful. Some such Western Buddhists have been steadfast in their commitment to their Buddhist practice for several decades, demonstrating a deep dedication. It is in this context that I am happy to see the publication of this new book *A Westerner's Introduction and Guide to Tibetan Buddhism*. Written by Sangak Tsomo, a long-time student and practitioner of Tibetan Buddhism, the book outlines the basic views of the Tibetan tradition and examples of some of its practices for the interested modern reader. I am pleased to note that while the author describes her personal journey into Buddhism in some detail, she continues to honor her traditional Jewish heritage.

I have no doubt that Western readers who wish to deepen their understanding of Tibetan Buddhist practices will find much to interest them here, and that members of other faiths, or even those who have none, will enjoy this sincere account of spiritual exploration.

June 6, 2014

Pema Khandro Ling
1221 Luisa Street, Suite A
Santa Fe, NM 87505
santafe@ewam.org

Ewam Sang-ngag Ling
PO Box 330 Arlee, MT 59821
406.726.0217 • www.ewam.org
admin@ewam.org

Nyingma School of Tibetan Buddhism

Gochen Tulku Sang-ngag Rinpoche
Spiritual Director

Foreword

For the benefit of Westerners who are beginners in the practice of Buddhism, Lama Tsomo has drawn on her own knowledge of Western and Eastern ways of thinking and devoted all her efforts to writing this current work, in order to provide a bridge that will forge a connection between these cultures. I am delighted that she has completed this book, and offer my sincere and heartfelt thanks and best wishes to her in this endeavor.

On this note, let me say a few words about Lama Tsomo, the author of this book, since she is a personal student of mine. Beginning with our initial meeting in 1995, she undertook the study and practice of the Buddhist teachings, including her spending two or three months each year in strict retreat, in addition to maintaining an uninterrupted daily practice. In this way, she has dedicated herself enthusiastically to completing a system of training from the preliminary stages up to and including the advanced yogic disciplines (*tsa-lung*) and Dzogchen practices.

On the basis of her efforts, in 2005 I formally recognized Lama Tsomo's accomplishments in an investiture ceremony that took place in conjunction with the graduation of the nuns who participated in the three-year retreat program at my meditation center of Kusum Khandro Ling in Pharping, Nepal.

Following this, in 2006, on the occasion of the final year of the intensive study program at Ewam Sang-ngag Ling in Arlee, Montana, I conferred on Lama Tsomo the formal title of a lama of the Ewam Foundation.

She has now authored this book to introduce people to the Buddhist teachings, in order to help new practitioners on into the future. I encourage all to read and study this text with a sense of trust in its usefulness, and am sure that they will profit greatly through such efforts. Please take this advice to heart.

This was written in my retreat cabin by the teaching throne of Longchenpa at Ewam Pema Khandro Ling, by me, the sixth holder of the title of Gochen Tulku.

Sang-ngag Tenzin
April 2014

~ Ewam Nepal ~
Turquoise Leaf Nunnery - Phone: 977-1-710-094/Sang-ngag Phurba Ling Retreat Center - Phone: 977-1-710-093
POB 7032 Devi G.B.S. Pharping Kathmandu, Nepal

Ewam is a federally registered 501(c)(3) US non-profit organization

WHO IS LAMA TSOMO?

And Why Should I Listen to Her?

As you read this book, and others in the series, you will come to know Lama Tsomo well: not just her teachings, but her "story"—the personal and spiritual path that led her to this book, and to you.

Before you begin, though, you may be curious about her credentials.

Lama Tsomo has spent a total of three years of strict, solitary retreat under the guidance of Tulku Sangak Rinpoche, during which time she progressed through all the stages of the Vajrayana path, the branch of Buddhism practiced in Tibet. In addition she has undergone thirty 1- to 2-week-long intensive trainings with Tulku Sangak Rinpoche and Khen Rinpoche. In 2005, Tulku Sangak Rinpoche ordained her as a lama in the Namchak tradition.

For a more thorough Curriculum Vitae please turn to page 126.

—Editor

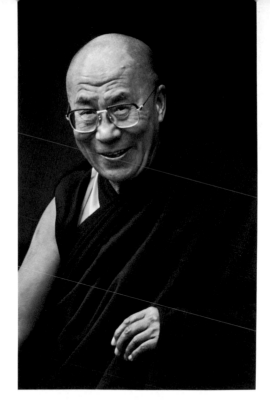

His Holiness the Dalai Lama XIV

PROLOGUE TO THIS SERIES

Tibetan Buddhist Practice—
Ancient Wisdom for Our Times

Whenever we see His Holiness the Dalai Lama, he always seems to be smiling and laughing. But in looking at His Holiness's life, we wouldn't automatically assume he's had reason to be happy all the time. He's had his share of serious health problems, for one thing. He's so happy and magnanimous all the time, that people forget he's a refugee. When China conquered his country in 1959, he fled for his life at the age that we usually graduate high school. He's lost his country, his people have suffered terribly, he has lived in exile, helpless as his people's culture and wisdom tradition are being systematically undone. And his crushing schedule would burn out people half—a *third*—his age.

Yet, smile he does. Constantly, joyfully. Hour after hour, year after year, no matter what happens. Although he is unquestionably a heavy-weight scholar and master practitioner, his constant joyfulness is palpable. His infectious laugh rolls out at the slightest provocation, and he jokes quite a bit, himself . . . then laughs at his own jokes!

This is not because he forgets the plight of his people, or sweeps his own suffering under the rug. When a nun, Ani Tenzin Palmo, spoke to him about the plight of women who had been trying to devote their lives to the *Dharma* with almost no support from the lamas, His Holiness burst into tears on the spot. He resolved that far greater opportunities had to be provided for women to reach the heights of scholarship and practice that men had been supported in pursuing.

Meanwhile, the sun came out shortly after that, and he was smiling again . . . while not forgetting his resolution. He has indeed—of course—followed through, and despite the challenge of changing age-old culture quickly, much progress has been made since then.

If you were to ask His Holiness why he smiles, of course I can't predict what he'd say. But judging from his writings and from witnessing him personally many times, I would say this:

He has plumbed the depths of understanding the nature of the universe and the nature of the mind. He has trained his own mind—both brain and heart. He has concluded that we are not separate from each other, as we so persistently think we are. I believe he lives within a view that holds the truth of our common root of being. He sees this as an ongoing reality, and stands in that reality.

Compassion, then, comes quite naturally if a person lives from that reality. And so does joy. He doesn't have to busy himself with "looking out for number one." (Or, to put it another way, the "one" he is looking out for is the "one" that is, ultimately, all of us.) Imagine that. What a *relief!* What *freedom.*

Every day, he spends several hours in our universal "home"—that great ocean of compassionate awareness. After his morning meditation, he sees with a clean lens everywhere he looks, so he perceives something close to the exquisitely beautiful *pureland* (heavenly realm) and pure inhabitants that are the true nature of things. Everything around him is alive. He sees each of us as another beautiful wave in the constant "dis*play*" of that great ocean. He sees the relatively tiny significance of his own wave-existence.

And remember, within and throughout that whole ocean . . . is *joy.* The kind we never have to depart from, even at death.

The Buddha has invited us home and shown us the way. Won't you come along?

Stupa garden at the Namchak Retreat Ranch

INTRODUCTION

Wisdom & Compassion (Starting with Yourself)

You probably know the old joke about the Manhattan tourist who asks a New Yorker, "How do you get to Carnegie Hall?" To which the reply is, "Practice, practice, practice!" So "How do you get to enlightenment?" "Practices, practices, practices!"

The first book in this Tibetan Buddhist practice series, *Ancient Wisdom for Our Times*, asked (and hopefully answered!) the question *Why Bother?* It laid a foundation of understanding for basic concepts in Tibetan Buddhism, as well as providing some history and personal and spiritual insights.

~~~~~~

If, as you read that book, the ideas made sense to you, I really recommend that you not leave it in the intellectual realm.* That's where this second volume comes in. The first book offered some ideas on *what* Tibetan Buddhism is and *why* its perspective and insights can be powerful. This volume begins to show you *how* to put that power into practice. Tibetan Buddhism isn't just a way of thinking, or feeling; it's a way of being and acting.

As I mentioned in *Why Bother?*, in my early experiences with Tibetan Buddhism, guided by Rinpoche, I was only at the stage of having road tested some of the methods and having liked the results so far. I wasn't necessarily ready for a full-on, lifelong commitment. So I was relieved by Rinpoche's reassurance that Tibetan Buddhism discouraged blind faith and in fact encouraged us to try out the methods for ourselves and see whether they worked for us, with our own experience as evidence and encouragement. I was a psychotherapist on my quest to find the world's best proven and provable methods for making myself and others better, happier people. If I could reach enlightenment, so much the better.

That said, when it comes to learning the practices, you'll want to gain some ability with the foundational ones before moving on to more advanced ones. You'll get far more enlightenment mileage out of exploring this text and related media, reading the recommended books, and doing the practices for about a year, than—for example—immediately forging ahead from one set of practices to the next.

Remember that understanding and mastery take time. Actually try the first practice for a while. Once you feel comfortable with that and have gained some benefit, you might feel ready to add the next one. While His Holiness the Dalai Lama has said that sooner or later everyone will reach enlightenment and "better it be sooner," racing through these practices will actually not get you there sooner. In fact, it would get you there much, much later (as in perhaps incalculable additional incarnations later).

So let's begin: patiently practicing and practicing patience.

_____

* And if you haven't yet read the first volume, I'd recommend you do so before proceeding with this one, so you'll have a framework for the practices we'll be working with.

Yum Chenmo statue, Garden of One Thousand Buddhas

METHODS SO WE CAN
SEE FOR OURSELVES

Checking Our Motivation

Someone once asked the Dalai Lama what the very first thing was that he did in the morning. He flashed his famous grin and shot back, "Check motivation!"

In Mahayana and Vajrayana, we have the Two Purposes the Buddha had: enlightenment for *self* and enlightenment for *others*. We want our sessions to be imbued with these Two Purposes. In other words, we want to be sure that our motivation for any practice—anything at all, actually—is compassion, *bodhicitta*.

In all of Mahayana and Vajrayana, it's very important to begin each day, as well as each practice session, by bringing that motivation to mind and making it stronger. If we infuse our practice with that motivation, the rubber really hits the road. If we don't, the brilliant, skillful means pretty much do nothing for us. Worse yet, our efforts won't go toward helping the billions of beings lost in Samsara, the *vast* majority of whom at this moment don't have the chance to progress toward enlightenment.

What can someone do toward liberation if they're in a bug body at this point, for example? And there are infinitely more beings incarnated in bug bodies than human ones. In this lifetime you and I happen to be humans, so we're on the front lines, with countless beings depending on us to make progress. When I'm sleepy in the morning and either feel like skipping the practice or just going through the motions, this thought is often the one that causes me to wake up and invest more of myself in the practice. I'm doing it for everybody else, too.

STUDENT   *What if my motivation isn't so good that morning?*

LT   I say this often, and I'll say it now: a practice session is a "come-as-you-are party."

On any given day, for any given practice, we do what we can at that moment to bring to mind all those beings who are depending on us. Most of them are far worse off than we are but can't do anything about it. Do we want to reach enlightenment just to save our own posterior portions? And never mind about the other poor suckers? Just remembering those other beings (and for the vast majority of my own incarnations, I've been every kind of creature other than human) often helps me. Compassion is a buddha quality because it's evidence that we feel ourselves to be one big awareness. That's why when someone hurts, we feel it.

Then again, if your motivation still isn't so great that morning, be compassionate with yourself. You're just a sentient being too, after all. Sometimes we have to "fake it till we make it." The important thing is to show up and do your best. (Woody Allen famously observed that "80 percent of success is just showing up"; of course, the other 20 percent is critical too.)

Fortunately this is only the first ushering-in to the practice. What follows—practices designed to bring forth compassion and mindfulness—will hopefully help. That's why we use all these skillful means, after all!

Now I'd like to ask YOU a question. What's a typical motivation for you, when you sit down to do a session?

STUDENT *Well, to be honest, it's often that I just want to slow my mind down and get it to focus better.*

LT Great. Why do you want to do that?

STUDENT *So I can function better.*

LT And what will that do? What are you looking for?

STUDENT *I'm looking to really be there when something good happens—not distracted. To do better work, stay on top of my interactions with my husband and kids . . . I mean, I'd like to be more aware, present, and compassionate for everything. I'm especially concerned that I be as compassionate as possible with my kids.*

LT So if you do better work, and are more aware and compassionate with those around you, what are you hoping will come of that? This may seem like a dumb question, but bear with me.

STUDENT *Okay. At work I know I could help so many people, if I make the right decisions and am really focused and present. Of course I love my kids and want to be the absolute best for them. And I hope that in the future, they will go out and benefit many people too. A lot of that depends on how I am with them. [Now with tears in her eyes] I guess my motivation, under all that, is really just to benefit beings after all.*

LT Yes. It was just a little covered over. Now you've really brought it forth. Now, imagine how much more powerful your meditation will be. So ask yourself these questions, and a couple of questions behind the questions, when you begin your day. And ask yourself again when you begin your meditation session too, if your motivation's not so great right when you wake up.

THE TIBETAN NOSE BLOW

The Theory

Okay, Tibetan Nose Blow is not the official name. It's my affectionate nickname for the practice we do to up our chances of really resting in still, clear, joyful awareness. In Tibetan it's called *Lung Ro Sel*, which is generally translated as "Clearing the Stale Energies."* We're speaking of subtle energies connected to the afflictive emotions—the Three Poisons.

---

* Sometimes described as "Clearing the Stale Winds."

The Tibetans are aware of subtle energy channels that run along either side of the spine, as well as a third one right up the middle. The side channels come up either side of the vertebrae in the neck, over each ear, and out each nostril. I bet you're already beginning to see why I call it the Tibetan Nose Blow, but let me continue.

A smoky, dirty blue, the middle channel is associated with *timuk*, the poisonous emotion category of ignorance, delusion, stupor, laziness, narrow-mindedness, and the like. We definitely want to clear *that* before trying to do practice!

The two on either side, as you may have guessed, are the other two passions, or poisonous emotions.

One is anything having to do with our yearning to draw to us the things and experiences that will make us happy. So *desire* and *clinging* are classic words used for this category.

The other one involves anything having to do with pushing away the things we *don't* want. Classic words for that category would be *aggression, hatred,* and *aversion.*

Desire is a smoky red, and aversion a smoky white. You're probably wondering why I'm not telling you which is on which side. I would be happy to, but I simply can't. It's different for different people. It's better if you come to it yourself, but it will still work even if you end up reversing them.

Here's how to tell: We each almost always have a favorite Poison. Some people tend to be very industrious but also tend to get frustrated quickly and have flare-ups of temper. They're obviously the ones who favor anger/aversion. Another example of someone with an affinity for this Poison—the smoky white channel—would be a very competitive person.

Those of you more partial to desire/longing/clinging might as well admit your tendency and go with the smoky red as your primary channel to clear. This happens to be my personal favorite. I used to hate to admit it and hoped nobody noticed. Now that I have so much experience in working with all of these Poisons in myself, the squeamish, judgmental reactions I used to have about my own tendencies are much, much smaller.

Tulku Sangak Rinpoche has taught that generally women have the red one (desire) on the right and the white one (aversion) on the left, while most men have that reversed. It's really not critical at this stage of training, so there's no need to worry about whether you've got it right. I guarantee you, you have all three, and you'll clear all three pretty well (at least temporarily) by the end of the Clearing of the Stale Energies.

STUDENT   *Every time I try to pick my favorite Poison or passion, I realize I also have the other one. In fact, one leads to the other. I'm angry at my husband because he won't turn off the TV and talk to me. That's because I desire him talking to me. If I weren't so stuck in my small way of thinking about things—ignorance—I wouldn't have a problem with the situation. So just in that one case, I have all three going on. How can I possibly decide?*

LT   You're absolutely right—one does lead to the other. That's part of what makes the Wheel of Samsara keep going around (and why it's not something more linear, like the golf course of Samsara). Of course we all have all three passions, so this isn't an exclusive decision. We're only talking about picking your favorite, the one that's most basic to your personality—your background color, you might say. Then we'll go ahead and clear *all three*—don't worry!

The Practice

Imagine the primary channel you want to clear on your right side, coming out your right nostril; the other, of course, on your left. And those of you whose favorite is ignorance/laziness/narrow-mindedness (the middle channel) can for now just go with your second favorite.

The methods of this exercise block the channels along which the karmic winds (karmic energies) run and clear out the neurotic emotions along the main three channels, leaving the energies (winds) of three of the Five Yeshes to arise in their place. We'll pull the spine really straight, to allow the yeshe winds to flow freely. We want those!

Each of the neurotic emotions (Three Poisons) has, at its very core, one of the yeshes. (In case you're wondering how we get from *Three* Poisons to *Five* Yeshes, I'll tell you. Under the general heading of anger there are two subcategories: pride and competitiveness/jealousy. This makes sense to me because both pride and jealousy have an aggressive quality about them.)

Pride and jealousy are associated with the remaining yeshes, Jewel and Karma.* So for this exercise, we'll work with the three major categories of afflictive emotions: the Three Poisons and their associated yeshes. Later I'll go deeper into the relationship between the yeshes and the Poisons, but for now I just wanted you to know a little bit about how this exercise works.

Once we've blocked the channels that could hinder our efforts, and cleared the neurotic energies/winds flowing through the others, the yeshe winds can come forth more fully. You can see why you'd want to take half a minute to accomplish *all that.* Everyone I know of who's tried this has found that it really does change their inner experience in just that short amount of time! Of course it's not a permanent change; that's why we do it before each practice . . . and then continue on to do the practice itself.

Now you're ready to "assume the position." No, not THAT position! The Seven Point Posture of Vairochana! If you can, get a firm cushion for your rear and sit on the floor or a mat; this helps to elevate the spine, causing it to tend to fall naturally into the right posture. Cross your legs with your feet on top of your legs, as you've all probably seen in yoga class or in most depictions of the Buddha—a yoga position called Full Lotus.

If you're young but not used to this sort of thing, please be gentle with yourself and slowly work your way into this posture over time. If you're older, all the more reason to be gentle with yourself. In time you may be able to do this too, but if not, it's not as though your chances for enlightenment are dashed! If you can sit cross-legged, or even with your feet in front of you, with knees to the side in some way, you can still do this exercise. Many people prop their knees up with small cushions. I hasten to remind you that you only have to hold the position for about half a minute. And, if all else fails, there's always the chair option—you can still reach enlightenment using the chair.

Now that you've woven your legs together, you're going to close some of those pesky channels that tend to carry the more neurotic karmic winds/energies. One of them runs through the base of your fourth finger. With each hand, you'll make a *vajra* fist by pressing your

---

* Please see glossary entries on the Five Dhyani Buddha Families, Five Poisons, and Five Primordial Yeshes, as well as the chart in the previous volume, *Why Bother?*

thumb against the base of your fourth finger and closing the rest of your fingers around it, forming a fist with your thumb inside. The one finger you leave straight is your index finger. You'll need that for covering your nostril.

Now you'll block other hindering, karmic channels that run through the hip joints. You'll curl your vajra fists under so that the backs of them are firmly placed on your legs, almost at the hip joint. Then you'll completely straighten your arms so that they're like poles.

STUDENT   *My arms are too long. There's no* WAY *I'll ever be able to straighten them.*

      LT   I thought the same thing. My arms are so long that most clothes are too short in the sleeves for me. To make matters worse, I'm short-waisted! Still, over time, and with a few helpful pointers, I've been able to hold that position for a half hour at a time. It's worth doing your best with this because you're using your arms to stretch your spine as straight as you possibly can. This allows the yeshe winds to flow more freely—worth the thirty seconds of effort, I'd say!

The Finer Points

To make it easier, you get to rotate the insides of your elbows toward the front. That, and having your seat elevated, will help. So will the slow process of just getting used to it.

Another tip is to let your shoulders come up by your ears. This is actually the official posture. Since a picture is worth a thousand words,

I've included some for you, if for no other reason than to show you that it's humanly possible!

So that's the Seven Point Posture of Vairochana. Now we're going to blow that smoky stuff out of the three channels in the spine area. Remember, whichever is your favorite—desire (smoky red) or aversion (smoky white)—put that one on the right side, to clear out first. If you're not sure, you can go with the convention that women generally have the red on the right and the white on the left; men the reverse.

Now lift the left fist, drawing a big, slow circle in the air with the index finger. Then place the index finger on your left nostril to block it off. Send that smoky stuff out your right nostril with a long, firm out-breath, ending with a strong push to get the last bit of air out. Imagine that the smoky-looking stuff is the neurotic aspect of the particular Poison, along with the thoughts that come from it. Include sickness on all levels, hindrances of various kinds, and obscurations of our true seeing—anything specific from the Poison you're working with. (Hopefully, nothing else of a more substantial nature will come out; just to make sure, I suggest blowing your nose before you start!)

Now put that fist back on the top of your leg, rotate your elbow as you straighten your arm, and do the same nose-blowing operation on the other side. You alternate the cleansing breaths three times, each time vividly imagining the channels becoming brighter and clearer. By the end, they're perfectly bright and clear, with their true essence

flowing through them: the red is Discerning Yeshe and the white is Mirrorlike Yeshe. When you peel away the drama and neuroses and get to their essence, you come to these two yeshes.

CLEARING ANGER: A PERSONAL STORY

Think of it: that sharp quality that anger has, if you take away the drama and neurosis, is a quality of Mirrorlike Yeshe. Years ago, a friend had repeatedly made plans to get together, then not shown up. I was angry. But insulating against the anger with "fluff" (ignorance, delusion), I had believed her excuses. One time, while I was doing a wrathful style practice, this old anger I'd forgotten about came bubbling to the surface. At that moment in meditation, I saw clearly how I was *still* holding a grudge toward that old friend I'd lost contact with many years before.

Had I really harbored anger in some corner of my mind? Unbelievable but true. How embarrassing! I used a powerful technique and the power of a great bodhisattva to clear the anger. What was left was compassion for the person . . . and crystal clarity about the situation, from her side and mine. I realized that actually we had very little to talk about. I hadn't lived in that place very long and hadn't found many friends, but really she wasn't someone I'd spend time with if there had been other choices. She'd lived there longer and had other choices.

I was able to stop being offended and just accept the truth of the situation. The whole thing was resolved in about twenty minutes. I was no longer in dullness, yet no longer carrying anger. With the help of the practice and my meditational deity (and the lama who brought all of that to me), I was able to drop the drama and come to the essence of Mirrorlike Yeshe, at least in this small way.

Likewise with desire, that emotion that continually says, "No, that's not quite it . . . I want THIS." Propelled by a longing that rarely has words, we continually chase after happiness, whatever that actually is. Imagine thumbing through a catalog, sometimes called a "wish book." Without the neurosis, as we navigate by the compass of knowing *true joy*, desire boils down to Discerning Yeshe.

If we took this clarifying process to its ultimate end, we would come to the place of ultimate, permanent happiness: Buddhahood. Our longing can actually serve as our compass, if we hold it lightly, peel away the layers of drama, and don't just try to assuage it with quick fixes near at hand.

We've all tried following the quick fixes and dog-earing the pages in our endless wish book, and it only brings us more Samsara. I must confess that I still do this, but after years of practice, I'm much more able to let go of the desire. By using my compass I've gotten better at finding my way to experiences that don't bring me more Samsara and instead actually leave me feeling more deeply fed.

Every arrow in the bow of desire
has rushed out in hope
of nearing
Him.
—SAINT THOMAS AQUINAS

Similarly, if we peel away the layers from the Poison of ignorance (smoky blue, in the middle), we go from dullness and delusion to the Yeshe of Basic Space (Dharmadatu); from stupor to timeless aware-ness *beyond* words. During that particular timeless half-hour epiphany in college I recounted in *Why Bother?*, my mind was awake and aware but not churning out thoughts. What I saw was beyond concepts. Some mornings, when I'm still in the stupor of sleep, I'm in the less-pure, ignorance end of that spectrum.

Back to the Blow by Blow

. . . so to speak. You've done six exhalations, alternating three on each side. With each out-breath, the once smoky red of desire and white of aggression got clearer and brighter. Now they're perfectly bright and clear red and white. Both fists are back on the tops of your legs with your arms straight, elbows rotated outward. Now you'll blow that smoky blue stuff out of the middle channel—three times out of both nostrils. Again, by the end it's bright, clear azure. What's left to flow through there is the Yeshe of Basic Space, the timeless awareness of that ocean of emptiness/awareness that's beyond/before thoughts and words. We go from stupor to wisdom beyond words. How lovely.

Now you gently exhale through the mouth and allow your hands to slide down your legs, unclenching your fists. They can just rest in a free position. The spine goes from firmly straight to a slightly relaxed, supple position—like a marionette hanging from a string. It's still straight, to allow the yeshe winds to flow freely, but with a flexible, floating quality.

Now rest for a moment or two in the new, lovely feeling you're no doubt experiencing. Since you've just cleared those channels that run through your nose, you don't want to stir them up again, so you breathe gently and naturally through your slightly open mouth. After the effort you just went to, why rush ahead? Surely you have another twenty seconds or so to experience this feeling, so relax a bit. Besides, it *feels good*. Sometimes I've got to admit that's been the best part of my practice session!

Neuroplasticity is on the cutting edge of brain science, so there are still many experiments to be done, but many have already clearly shown the benefits of meditation through functional magnetic resonance imaging (fMRI), electroencephalography (EEG), double-blind studies, and other objective methods.

One such study was on attention-deficit/hyperactivity disorder (ADHD) in both adults and adolescents, many of whom had this disorder in its genetic form. After doing Shamata (Tranquil Abiding) Meditation for just five to fifteen minutes a day for a few months, they showed marked improvement! Imagine if those of us without ADHD did the same thing.

SCIENCE TIDBIT
Modern Science and Meditation

"Mindful awareness promotes neural integration."

Contemplative Science—the field that studies the effects of meditation—is new, but it's already surprisingly large, and growing larger. More and more universities across the globe are conducting studies in this area, most of which reveal various marked benefits of meditation. So far, we've mostly had to be satisfied with inklings and tantalizing tidbits gleaned from this or that experiment. In *The Mindful Brain*, psychiatrist, scientist, educator, and meditator Daniel Siegel (quoted above) shows us not just the whether, but also tantalizing hypotheses as to *how*.

Given his background and experience, Siegel is in a particularly good position to put the science, clinical evidence, and meditation experience together in an understandable, sensible, and exceedingly helpful way. I found that not only did most of his hypotheses make sense to me, but if we really accept them, we realize just how powerfully we could use them to change our lives.

In the beginning of the book, Siegel gives us an anatomy lesson on the human brain, takes us with him on his "Meditation Retreat for Scientists," and then weaves back and forth between brain functions and what I'll call mind functions. He makes this distinction, and connection, clear

Fortunately, we don't have to imagine. Another study compared longtime meditators with "normal" non-meditators and found that the meditators had vastly more capacity to hold their attention on the object of their choice.

But what about those of us who won't be living in a cave for thirty years so we can devote ourselves to daily practice? Will we get any noticeable benefit with much less meditation? A three-month study at the University of California, Davis, worked with subjects with some meditation experience, but not "super-meditators" who had been practicing for decades or meditating extensively every day. The study participants were measured before, during, and after a three-month retreat. Though participants

through intriguing statements such as "The mind can actually use the brain to create itself." He shows us how that might work.

Through objective observation—his review of his own and others' laboratory experiments—together with his subjective experience in learning a form of Tranquil Abiding Meditation, Siegel has developed intriguing theories about how our meditation practice changes us both mentally and physically, affecting even how we relate to other people. As with the work of other scientists, the implications are huge.

He brings us current scientific knowledge of what takes place in which parts of the brain, and how these parts work together across regions. He goes on to show how both the regions and the "wires" connecting them can change function and size depending on how we *use* our brains. For most of the history of neuroscience, it was accepted that the brain didn't change after early childhood. But in recent decades, more and more experiments have proved unquestionably that our brains do change throughout our lives.

The term for this newly acknowledged capacity of the brain is *neuroplasticity*, the brain's ability to change how many neurons do which jobs, the number of blood vessels in a particular area, and the nature and number of lines of communication between parts of the brain. All of these changes together can create a whole new map of brain functionality in the same person, over the months and years. The saying "Use it or lose it" applies even on this level!

couldn't always match the scores of more experienced meditators, they did achieve steady, significant improvement over the three months.

Participants were tested on a variety of attributes, including focus, attention span, and longevity factors that can be measured through blood tests that reflect cellular aging—the wear and tear on the body that can be exacerbated by stress—at the outset of the retreat, halfway through, at the end, and five months after that. Not surprisingly, their beginning scores were the same as those of the control group who weren't on the retreat. Halfway through, though, the meditators had improved markedly on all tests. By the end they were doing even better, while the control group stayed the same. (Before you feel too bad for the control group, be reassured that they got to do the next three-month retreat/study.)

But what happened once the meditators went back to their normal lives? They were tested again after five months, and their changes held! They were still doing shorter daily meditation sessions, but those didn't take up much time in their busy lives.

Let's take a look at one of the key factors: concentration. During the retreat, the meditators were given a difficult, though intentionally boring, challenge that required intense concentration and comparative

analysis. As the retreat continued, the meditators were able to concentrate, and perform, better and better on this task. Again, those improvements held long after the retreat was over. This study suggests that an intensive meditation "boot camp" has immediate, increasing, and lasting benefits.

But what about those of us who don't happen to have three months free? In a much shorter and less intensive study reported in *Time* magazine, scientists at the University of North Carolina at Charlotte found that after only four days of meditation training for just twenty minutes a day, students showed impressive improvement on a variety of cognitive-skills tests. On a timed information-processing test designed to induce deadline stress, the meditators did significantly better than the controls. On a particularly challenging computer test that measured sustained attention, the brand-new meditators did *ten times* better than the control group! Who wants to be in the control group? If schools are supposed to train our minds, why are we not teaching this in all schools? And why wait until university?

There are many other such examples of improvement: in attention span, focus, and "visual discrimination"; in many longevity factors, such as relaxation; and even in compassion (yes, they found ways to

measure compassion). What are we to make of such brain changes, beginning even after four days of short meditation sessions?

For one thing, this means that experience puts its stamp on the brain. And, taking advantage of neuroplasticity by carefully setting up a well-designed experience and repeating it again and again, we will increase the size of some of the brain's "real estate," as well as the blood vessels feeding it and the links to other parts of the brain. In all of the practices in Tibetan Buddhism, we're *choosing* carefully crafted experiences, honed over thousands of years, with huge numbers, designed specifically to make these changes in the best, most efficient way.

Speaking in general terms, Siegel says that before learning meditation, most of us take in sensory information from the outside world, associate that information with similar memories, and then act on that association. For example, if we meet a new person whose face reminds us of a grumpy schoolteacher we had trouble with, we might try to avoid that person or be more guarded or defensive toward our hapless new acquaintance. Siegel refers to this method of processing as "top-down" because within the geography of the brain, the parts activated in such processes are triggered in a more or less vertical progression.

By contrast, when we use specific parts of the brain associated with what Siegel calls "Executive Attention," characterized by "effortful control" in balance with sensory parts, memories, and others, we operate in more of a wheel shape, with a hub (region in charge of Executive Attention and its close relatives), spokes (neural pathways to other regions), and rim (sensory information regions). Siegel shows how brain anatomy corresponds to this process, with the center of Executive Attention at the hub.

In other words, our brain is built to work either way: top-down or like a wheel. You can see how giving voluntary, or "Executive," Attention such a central role can help us be not only more skillful in our responses, but more free—less a prisoner to past experiences, doomed to repeat them again and again. Think of the lady who reminded us of the grumpy schoolteacher. If we behave badly toward her, how is she likely to behave toward us? Around and around we go.

Repeated meditation, over the course of months or years, increasingly helps us to move from the vertical, knee-jerk process to the more intentional, free, and resourceful wheel process.

Contemplative Science goes on to show that we *sustain* changes catalyzed by meditation even after we get up off the cushion. Once the pathways and processes are set, the new way of functioning becomes the default way of dealing with all experience. The old synapses (pathways) gradually diminish, some even disappearing after months and years of disuse. Through repeated use, the new ones go from footpaths, to streets, to thoroughfares.

Many experiments have shown that the techniques of Tibetan Buddhism help us put just the right paths between just the right parts of the brain, and balance them in just the right way, so that we can let go of knee-jerk reactions and have compassionate, balanced, resourceful, and constructive responses to experiences—and people—that come our way.

In his book, Siegel maps all this out in detail, citing some of the studies on Tibetan Buddhist meditators. I've included some others here as well. Though I don't agree with all of Siegel's hypotheses, I have to say that I've found many of them (and those of Contemplative Science) to be true for me, as well as for most of my students. Speaking from their subjective experience, almost all of my students have reported being better able to handle painful experiences with less stress, and having more mastery over challenging interactions with others. They also report a generally heightened sense of well-being, with greater capacity for love, joy, and compassion. I would report the same for myself.

But the benefit of the practices doesn't stop there. The knee-jerk mental process also produces endless chatter. Anyone who's spent ten minutes trying to meditate knows that! Siegel takes us with him on his first meditation retreat, which was the mental equivalent of going from couch potato to marathon boot camp. At first he went "a little stir-crazy," finding the long sessions weird and uncomfortable.

After a huge inner struggle, he was soon able to drop that internal conversation for at least a few minutes, or the duration of a meditation session. Then this newfound clarity and focus began to persist even on breaks between sessions. He was now free to really *feel* the cool breeze on his face, really *see* the forest around him: free to allow the heart-rending beauty of the moment to penetrate him. The first time that happened fully, he burst into tears.

Connecting

Not only have I spent most of my life separated from experience by my internal monologue, I've dampened my emotions to protect myself from feeling. When I was about thirteen, I thought, "If I could just feel the good things in life and not feel the bad, wouldn't that be great?" After numbing myself till my life was in black and white, I realized I was living in a state of mild depression. Everything was gray and two-dimensional—like I was looking at life instead of actually living. I would go to the mountains and only experience the beauty and vastness as though I were sipping from a waterfall through a straw. The exquisite mountain was fully there, but I wasn't.

Through body-centered psychotherapy, I began to feel everything more fully again. Through Tibetan meditation practices, I've been able to let go of the unhappy feelings—let go of all lingering thoughts/feelings from the past, conjecture about the future—so that I can REALLY feel what's happening in the moment. As the saying goes, "God is here; where are you?"

When I'm having a difficult interaction with someone, I'm more able to manage my responses and freer to respond more kindly, resourcefully, and ultimately successfully. I'm by no means perfect, but the vast improvement is obvious to me as well as others who have known me for a long time.

But there's yet another experience that comes with letting go of the top-down way of processing life. We're no longer prisoners of the self we thought we were. Once we're operating more from the hub of the wheel, we're not just a composite of memories and habitual reactions. Those memories are there, but with hours of meditation experience, we don't identify so tightly with those memories and habitual patterns. We're able to open up to what the Contemplative Scientists are calling the *ipseity* sense of ourselves, a more basic sense of being that Siegel likens to the Theravada Buddhist term "bare awareness." Perhaps pointing at the same phenomenon, Thich Nhat Hanh, a famous Vietnamese Zen master, refers to "interbeing."

In my experience, I drop or suspend my personality to an extent, and am able to sink to a more profound level beneath it, which I simply call awareness. Because I have this awareness in common with everyone else, this helps immensely with my ability to join with others. I feel joined with all things, all creations within the one great awareness.

It's much easier to be moral—natural, really—when coming from this place. Just as when I stub my toe, my whole self experiences it, so from the point of view of "me" being the whole ocean, when one being suffers, I suffer too.

In meditation I often feel free of my usual sense of self, but it's more than that. I feel that my awareness goes beyond my skin. Siegel invented the term *transpirational integration*, meaning that as the different regions of the brain relate in this balanced way, there is a sense of "breathing across" the different regions. This can extend into a breathing across from one human to another, one human to all creation.

So this psychiatrist has perhaps begun to point at *how*, in the brain, we're able to *feel* this universal truth that's been expressed for ages, from Sufi poetry to Hildegard von Bingen's revelations, to the mystics of all religions. In Buddhism we say that without the constructed self in the way, we can experience the one vast awareness that I'm calling Buddha Mind. There is no more immediate, no truer perception of reality than that. And nothing more satisfying and joyful. It's the ultimate experience of *coming home.*

So if your goal is to be healthier, smarter, better (i.e., more compassionate and skillful) and ultimately happier, you now know that this set of methods is scientifically endorsed!

Instructional video for this practice is available at Namchak.org

TRANQUIL ABIDING

My experience is what I agree to attend to.

—WILLIAM JAMES[*]

Shamata

There are a few things I really like about the practice of Shamata, which translates from Sanskrit as "Tranquil Stillness," or "Peaceful Abiding." I like the term *Tranquil Abiding*, because when we Westerners start doing this practice, we tend to demand that our minds suddenly be still. We think meditation means sitting there and thinking of nothing for a half hour. The emphasis for me,

---

[*]   *The Principles of Psychology*, Volume I

though, is the tranquility of the experience. *Shiney*, the Tibetan term for Shamata, literally means "Tranquil Abiding."

I also like how very restful Shamata can be, as its name implies. We tend to spend all day relating to people and things outside ourselves. Even if we aren't actively relating to them *out there*, we're thinking about them *inside* ourselves, in between, in our thoughts and feelings. Even at night, in our dreams, our minds are busy. Even when we finally get to sit on the beach. Even between lifetimes.

We've chased after thoughts, following them with the next thoughts, following those with words and actions . . . for an eternity. Wouldn't it be nice to take a break from making these movies all the time? To take a REAL break, and just *rest*? I get exhausted just at the thought of how long I've been ceaselessly dashing around, mentally or physically. We all need a vacation, right? Well, I take a *real* one every day—in my morning practice session!

And what makes it especially nice is that I get to *officially* do nothing and be *virtuous* in the bargain! No answering the phone, no thinking about work, no deciding what to do about dinner, no solving the vexing problems in my life—whew! No wonder doctors recommend forms of meditation for high blood pressure. I know some women who do it just to slow the aging process. Scientists have found that meditation boosts the immune system for many hours afterward.

And because I don't have to do or think about anything on the outside during Shamata, I can turn the lens inward, at last. I can just sit with my mind. In doing this simple practice, I've learned more about the true nature of my mind and how it works than in all my years of studying psychology. For all the reasons the Buddha has taught us, we might as well know what's really going on in there so we can go about straightening it out . . . or even just to *know*. (As the New Testament says, "You shall know the truth, and the truth shall make you free.")

I don't know about you, but I'm *curious*—fascinated, even. And if I run into something I want to change, I have the methods to do it. But during Tranquil Abiding, we don't even have to direct our thoughts or come up with diagnoses and remedies. That comes in other practices. Here we just see them and remain, well, tranquilly abiding. After all this running around, reacting to outer phenomena all our lives (and countless others), we haven't ever just sat with our minds and observed them. What better way to learn the nature of our minds? If we want to refine something, we first need to know the nature of the thing.

As I've said, many modern people think we have to make our minds stop thoughts altogether during meditation. But the brain is, among other things, a thinking machine. It's okay to leave the machine on and let thoughts come and go. The problem comes when we chase after these thoughts and make whole movies about them. *That is the cause of our suffering.* The Buddha saw exactly how that works, and I've shared some of his explanation. As you sit in Shamata, you'll see those dynamics in action, for yourself.

I've noticed a big catch-22 with these practices. We're using the impure mind to work on the mind. So if the tool is imperfect, won't the results be imperfect? That's why we begin with Shamata. We need to refine the tool. Meanwhile, we will already begin, in the process, to get to know the nature of our minds.

There's another catch-22, and at one point I asked Rinpoche about it. Many of the practice texts say that if you do a practice perfectly, and your mind doesn't waver for a moment, and you perceive everything in just the right, enlightened way, you can reach enlightenment by doing that practice. But if I could do the practice that way, I'd already *be* enlightened, and I wouldn't need to do the practice! I pointed this out to Rinpoche, who smiled, knowing all about this, and said, "We keep on doing the practice, and little by little, it will distill our minds so that we will reach the goal after all."

There's yet another important reason for doing Tranquil Abiding. I think we'd all like to be better able to focus our minds on something and have it stay there. We can all do it sometimes, for a short time, but what if your mind became more dependably really peaceful and stable? I'm not talking about sinking into a stupor; quite the contrary. When we're doing good Shamata, our minds are resting in their true state, which is bright, clear, and vivid. Wouldn't *that* be a nice way to start or end the day—resting in clear, vivid awareness?

I've always wanted to fully experience a beautiful moment, like the sun painting the clouds with pastel light at sunset. But my mind was so constantly lost in its movies that I could never be fully there; now I can. Of course the sunset is fully available to you. With some practice at this technique you can fully be there for it too.

When we do Shamata long-term, our minds become more supple, even as they become more stable. This is not a rigid practice; it's a very gentle one. It wouldn't be very restful if it were rigid, would it? Masters who have done a lot of this and other practices for years find that they need very little sleep. It seems that the rejuvenating effects of such practices are more efficient than normal sleep. Who wouldn't like *that* fringe benefit?

Yet another reason to do Shamata—and this one is essential—is that without that ability to put our mind on something and have it stay there, how can we get any serious benefit from the other practices? If our minds can't stay on the mantra or the visualization, no matter how brilliantly the practice is engineered, it can't do us much good. That's why, even though this is the main practice of Theravada (School of the Elders), we also begin with this practice in Vajrayana. As you can probably see, it's foundational. Sure, we'll go on to build the walls and the roof, but first let's lay a good foundation so the house really serves us well.

The Actual Practice of Tranquil Abiding— A Brief Introduction

Now that you've brought forward your bodhicitta motivation and done the Tibetan Nose Blow, you're in a *much* better frame of mind to do this practice.

Now you can begin the main part. Sit with your back in that supple-yet-straight position. Your pelvis is rotated slightly forward, with your lower belly hanging forward a bit. If you can sit cross-legged on a firm cushion, that's ideal. Almost cross-legged, with one foot in front, is also good. If not, a chair with a firm seat is fine too. In that case I'd recommend a thin, small, firm cushion at the small of your back. There are lots of orthopedic back support gadgets out there that work well. You could give them a try.

Another option that I happen to be fond of, because of a hip problem, is what I call the "knees-up" position. I sometimes alternate it with the cross-legged position. Sitting on the floor on a firm cushion, you put your feet together and your knees up. You can wrap your arms around your knees and clasp your hands together for support. For this position, I like to use the *gom tak*, a Tibetan meditation belt. It's a band of felt that wraps around your back as well as your knees. Generally it's nearly four inches wide; the length depends on your size. You can buy these from some Dharma stores online (ours, for one!). Some students have simply used a very large, wide belt.

Whichever position you choose, the main point is that your back has to be straight, without strain.

Your shoulders should be back. Your hands are typically folded, one on top of the other, palms facing up, in your lap. If that gets to be hard on your shoulders (I tend to slump, so I'm in this category), you can let your hands rest farther down each leg, close to the knees. I have my palms facing down, but Rinpoche doesn't seem to be too strict on this point.

If you're a marionette hanging from the ceiling, with the string coming out the top/back of your head, your chin naturally comes down a bit. As a matter of fact, your jaw is slack and slightly open. Your teeth and lips don't quite meet, and you're breathing very gently through your mouth. (After clearing our nostrils through Lung Ro Sel, a.k.a. the Tibetan Nose Blow, we don't want to stir the karmic winds up again!) The tip of your tongue just touches the place where your upper teeth meet the roof of your mouth.

Your eyes are in a downward gaze, only half-open. Your breath wafts in through your mouth and your belly swells as it comes in—like filling a wineskin—filling from bottom to top. On the out-breath, you reverse the process, letting the air out from top to bottom.

Some Shamata Tips

STUDENT   *In other meditation classes, I've learned to close my eyes in*
meditation. I like that. Can I just go ahead and close my eyes?

LT   Rinpoche has taught me from his lineage, and there are all
kinds of differences in technique from lineage to lineage.
One reason to have the eyes half-open is that when
they're closed, we can more easily go off on some fantasy
or train of thought. We're also more likely to settle into a
stupor or even nod off to sleep. We don't want to fall into
either mental meanderings or stagnation in our practice.
We tend to go from one to the other in life, and we're
trying to do something quite different here. As Mingyur
Rinpoche would put it, the key is to . . . *rest, but not get lost.*

We're going for . . . *vivid, joyful stillness.*

Rinpoche has taught me to keep my eyes open to let
the light in. That seems to help achieve that vivid, joyful
stillness. As Ram Dass famously advised us . . .

Be . . . here . . . now.

Rinpoche has also pointed out that the aim of
Vajrayana is to join the state achieved in practice with
everyday life. We're laying that foundation when we keep
our eyes a bit open, allowing the
apparitions of this world to remain

Be . . . here . . . now.   within our eyesight, while we rest
our minds in the underlying reality.

Eventually we want to master joining both realities—the
ocean and its waves, the Two Truths—in our view. He has
said that keeping the eyes open is also better preparation
for Dzogchen, the highest level in Tibetan Buddhism.

STUDENT   *Is it okay to play background music while I do Shamata?*

LT   Alas, no. Though it could be pleasant, it would detract
from this particular mind training you're pursuing.

STUDENT   *I can sit cross-legged on a cushion, which I'd like to do, but after a*
while my foot falls asleep.

LT   Many of us have had that problem. Me too. A few tips can make a big difference. One is to make sure your cushion is very firm. If you're sinking into your cushion, it's much more likely you'll cut off your blood supply. The other advice is to sit right on your sit-bones, moving the, er, flesh out of the way as you sit down. Then you're moving the blood vessels out of the way too. Also, unlike the Theravada version of this, if you need to move in the middle of your session because your foot is falling asleep, you may. At that point you might want to switch to the knees-up position.

STUDENT   *I've noticed many meditation traditions have us focus on our breath. What's the reason for this?*

LT   There are probably several, and the short answer is, I don't know. I do know from personal experience that it helps me to settle into a more alert yet calm state, with a minimum of distraction—relatively speaking!

  When I looked up *inspiration* in the *Oxford English Dictionary*, it was defined in two ways. One was "inhalation"; the other, "divine influence." Why would those two meanings be embedded in our language? What unconscious understanding let us see those as related? We also speak of the "breath of life," not referring just to a biological need for oxygen.

Now we'll do twenty-one breaths as a deeper ushering-in to the session. Again, the air floats gently through our mouths, swelling our lower bellies first. Then it fills the rest of our trunks. We pause as long as is comfortable, then exhale. Gentle pause again. That's one. Continue that way till you've done twenty-one of those. I like to use my *mala* to count. I put a marker bead at number twenty-one on my mala, then go to the large "guru bead" so I don't have to count to get to it every time. You can always repeat the twenty-one breaths anytime during your session.

When we practice Shamata, we're spending a few minutes out of the twenty-four hours of breathing we do in a day being *aware* of—*present for*—our taking in of the divine and being affected and sustained by it. What better foundation for mindfulness practice? What better ushering-in to the tranquil state we're seeking?

Clearing the Stale Energies bases its methodology on the understanding that thoughts and emotions ride the breath. Using the breath, we clear away those unwanted thoughts and emotions. Now we let the breath come in, naturally, tranquilly, while focusing our intention and attention on the breath itself. This makes sense to me.

Harking back to *The Mindful Brain*, Siegel notes that our breathing is operated by both the automatic and intentional parts of our nervous systems; unconscious and conscious; body and mind. How interesting, to sit on that cusp while practicing mindfulness and tranquility.

Shamata: The Main Event

Now we're really into the main part. In the first months you'll want to use an "object of support," as it's called. Think of it as training wheels. I sure appreciated them when I was learning to ride a bike! As you practice, have a picture or statue of an enlightened being in your line of sight (remember: your eyes aren't closed!). An example would be the Buddha Shakyamuni, the founder of Buddhism. Another would be Guru Rinpoche, who brought Vajrayana Buddhism to Tibet and reached full Buddhahood himself. Another would be his consort Yeshe Tsogyal, and another would be their Great Mother figure, Green Tara, or any of the twenty-one Taras that emanate from her, for that matter. Remember our discussion in *Why Bother?* on the power of images—archetypal ones, in particular.

In case you don't happen to have such an image handy, I've included one in the packet at the back of this book. It's Vajradhara, which, according to the Nyingma tradition, is the *Sambhogakaya*-level (the archetypal) form of the primordial Buddha. It's in *yab-yum*, which means "in both its male and female forms, in union." This symbolizes the union of the realized masculine and feminine principles: awareness/emptiness, wisdom/skillful means, wisdom/compassion, and many others.

I do find it beautiful and evocative. To me they're like the original father and mother—the ones we all wish we'd had, but we had neurotic sentient beings for parents instead (of course, they had us—neurotic sentient beings—for kids, so it evens out). I love my parents, but of course they're imperfect. Beholding the pure forms evokes something very healing for me. If you're going to stare at something for hours, it might as well be beautiful, evocative, and inspiring.

New science has found that images registered in the retina go immediately to the amygdala, an almond-sized/shaped part of our brain. The amygdala is sometimes likened to an orchestra conductor. Built for survival, it instantly sends its interpreted messages to whatever parts of the brain it's programmed to send them to. Since survival trumps everything else, so do the messages of the amygdala.

For example, we're walking down a forest path. Suddenly our heart starts to pound and we jump to the side. Only later do we realize we'd seen a stick out of the corner of our eye. The amygdala associated the twisted, oblong shape with "snake" and sent messages to the heart and legs before our conscious mind in the cerebral cortex had a word to say about it. As scientific studies have shown, it hadn't even gotten the message yet. Later we can take the time to decide if it's really a snake and think about what to do. Our survival programming gives us the luxury of that time, which in hunter-gatherer days meant life or death.

The Tibetans may not have known about the amygdala, but they sure understood the immediacy of imagery and how it engages all levels, conscious and unconscious. Jung did extensive experiments on association and proved that our brains work almost entirely on association. He based many of his theories on that knowledge.

One student *insisted* on meditating on a penny that he'd whip out of his pocket and toss on the ground in front of him. Even after I'd explained why an enlightened being might be a tad more inspiring, he stuck with his penny as his meditative support. In fact he became more insistent. Oh well. I practiced patience. It was his choice, after all. Many months went by, until he announced one night that he couldn't imagine why he'd want to meditate on money. For many years he'd been dedicated to a life free from worrying about money. Why meditate on a penny—especially when he was having some hard times financially. Why, indeed? It would have been un-Buddhist to say "I told you so." So I didn't.

After you've taken your twenty-one breaths, keep your gaze steadily resting on the image in front of you.

THOUGHT EXPERIMENT

To give yourself a sense of how you're affected by imagery, I invite you to take a moment to be your own scientist. Please stop and remember a scary scene in a movie. Maybe a malevolent person or creature was sneaking up behind our hero or heroine. How did you feel in that moment? Most of us feel anxious, our hearts beating faster, our breath short, eyes wide, almost as if it were happening to us in real life. Now zero in on your memory of the "bad guy's" face. Do you feel warm and fuzzy? I doubt it. What are you feeling?

Now rest your gaze on the face of Guru Rinpoche or White Tara. What qualities do you see there? What feelings arise in you? Please jot them down.

All of these—the "bad guy," Guru Rinpoche, White Tara—are archetypal images that we tend to associate with certain qualities and that tend to evoke corresponding feelings. Why not use the positive images to help us rouse the positive thoughts and feelings we want to cultivate in our lives? Scientists are only just now beginning to discover the effects of imagery throughout the depths and breadth of the brain. Tibetan practices, in particular, make use of this phenomenon in a highly refined way. So, as Tibetan Buddhists have known for centuries and as

modern scientists are also discovering, there are good reasons for us to use an image of an enlightened being in our practice. Perhaps in this little experiment, you've begun to get an inkling.

Now What?

Well, here you are, having "assumed the position" for Tranquil Abiding, *looking like* a buddha, and hopefully *breathing* like a buddha, while looking *at* a buddha.

The main point of the whole exercise is what you do with your *mind*. The answer? Nothing.

Rest in your truly natural state: joyful, heartful, alive, and relaxed. That's it. I'm not kidding. Oh, if only our minds would do that for a nice, long time!

Mind in Agitated State

Once, long ago, a man received a wonderful present from a master: a magical monkey that could do anything the man asked of it. Well, of course he was thrilled! He took the monkey along with him and asked it to do all sorts of useful things. In no time at all, it would finish each task and come running back for the next order. The man had the monkey build him a palatial house. In no time at all, the monkey had finished it. Now our friend was *really* thrilled. What's not to like?

The man went to bed for the night and found out. The monkey kept pestering him, "NOW what do you want me to do? What next?" The man could never rest, ever! Day and night the monkey hounded him with requests for more work, which it finished in no time. Then it was back for more.

At his wits' end, the man went back to the master. "Help! You've *got* to give me a way to deal with this monkey so that it doesn't keep on bothering me day and night! What can you do?!"

The master gave him one curly hair. He intoned, "Have the monkey make the hair go straight." The master demonstrated pulling the hair straight. As soon as he let go, the hair bounced back to its former shape. That was it. The man took the hair and gave it to the monkey, ordering it to make the hair straight. The monkey sat down, fully focused on the little hair. He pulled it straight. It bounced back. He pulled it again. It bounced back again. So it went for about a minute. The man raced to his bed and gratefully passed out.

This story was from the days before straightening irons.

Many Buddhists refer to the "monkey mind," and now you know why. Our discursive mind is like the mind of that monkey: it serves us well but never gives us a moment's rest. Even at night we're living out dramas and working out problems in our dreams. Great masters who rest in the clear light of basic awareness need very little sleep—and I daresay they get more rest!

Our meditative support acts like the curly hair. After lifetimes of busily dashing after thoughts, if we ask the mind to suddenly "take five," how could it possibly do that? If we ask a puppy to do a "down-stay" for an hour in the first lesson, we're going to have a very unhappy puppy and owner. It simply ain't gonna happen. We'd do well to give it a bone to chew on. It still won't stay for an hour, but it'll stay for a bit.

I don't know of any Theravada or Mahayana Lineages that use an image as a meditative support in the way that we do, but I like the fact that Vajrayana does, in the beginning. As I've tried one after another Vajrayana practice, I've found these practices very realistic in meeting our minds as they are NOW. From that starting point, the practices lead us to loftier, more rarified states. The higher the level of practice, the stronger the medicine, until you're experiencing some really amazing things. Most important, your mind has really changed. If we try to start at the lofty places, though, the mind will be like that fidgety untrained puppy being asked to do a "down-stay" for an hour.

Remember that you're not expected to sit there and think of nothing for the whole time. Again, that's not realistic. But many Westerners beginning meditation do make this mistake, drive themselves crazy in the attempt, and get discouraged and/or give up. If, as we meditate, thoughts arise and fall away, like waves in the ocean, no problem. That's reality. Empty awareness gives rise to appearances, and thoughts are a kind of appearance. If we could let well enough alone . . . we wouldn't be in this mess of a movie we call Samsara. The Buddha also saw the appearances, but he didn't have to do or think anything about them, so he could let them be.

But rarely can we let well enough alone. Because we identify with one apparition, "me," ego, we have a vested interest in following the course of this movie, in which we are both audience and the main character.

SIGNING UP FOR SAMSARA BY THE NANOSECOND

A thought arises and we grab hold of it.

We generate another thought in response to that one, perhaps embellishing our thought in pursuit of something we desire, or perhaps changing the subject in an effort to push away an unwanted experience.

And on and on and on it goes, one thought tumbling after another, all spurred on by "needs" of our afflictive emotions. We want to attract this thing we're thinking of, and push away that other thing.

All those internal conversations you have going on, oh, once in a while. The endless problem-solving, as you try to figure out how you can get that promotion, push that difficult person out of your way, make someone like you back, etc., etc., etc.—*that's* not letting well enough alone. That's not Tranquil Abiding. We sign up for Samsara every moment, involved with the movie, jumping in and starring in it, trying to produce, direct, rescript, and recast it as it flows by. We could stop at any frame, but we don't even notice that there are separate frames, or even that it's a movie.

Let's look at this chain reaction in slow motion. You're sitting there, meditating, breathing and gazing peacefully. The thought of your manager at work pops up. Yesterday she told you she didn't like your clever idea. You see her face in your mind's eye. You hear her dismissive tone. NOW is the moment you could simply be aware of that thought and let it pass. But in a less-than-mindful moment, with frustration (the little

brother of anger/aversion) in your heart, you jump to the next link in the chain reaction. You think of what you'd say back to her, trying different sentences, imagining how she responds. Then you decide maybe it would be better to go over her head and tell her manager or to get your fellow workers to join you in putting your idea forward. The more you spin these scenarios, the more agitated, and less peaceful, you feel.

You see how this plays out: now you've got a whole movie going on, and you're the star. And there is nothing tranquil or abiding about this production.

And maybe, at some point in your revved-up agitation, you remember: "Oh, yeah, I was meditating."

The drama started not with the image and words of your manager, actually, but with your *following after that thought*. And in that moment you went from peace to Samsara. This is how we sign up for Samsara every minute, every day.

We commonly say, "You made me mad." Well, Rinpoche probably felt like saying that to the guards when he first got to prison. But then he learned that, whatever the guards did or whatever situation he was in, *his own reaction was quite another thing*. This uncoupling of outer goings-on from our reactions to them is key to our finding peace. If we're dependent on everything being just right in our outer world, it's going to be a long wait (and by *long*, I mean infinite), so we'll never find happiness. Gaining the ability to respond as we wish to is the only way I can imagine to be happy all the time. It's also the way to true freedom.

If we don't have any personal (ego) stake in what happens when a face and words pop up, then they very quickly vanish, without any drama. In Vajrayana we sometimes speak of a thief coming to an empty house. There's no point in staying. So if we become a dispassionate observer—not numbed out but simply without indulging in that "personal stake"—these thoughts, appearances, even feelings can come and go in an endless flow, and we haven't lost our seat. Under these circumstances, gradually the flow of thoughts will naturally slow down. We can experience the true nature of our minds, see to the depths, only once the waters have been stilled.

Even in the early stages of Shamata practice, I found I could experience a bit of stillness in the pause between breaths. I found I would lengthen that pause a little, to savor that lovely stillness. You might try that yourself, without pushing or making a big effort out of it. Just a little pause.

In the gap between two thoughts,
Thought-free wakefulness manifests unceasingly.
—MILAREPA

YOUR MIND WORKING ON YOUR MIND—CATCH-22? A LITTLE.
At this point, let's face it: we can't do pure Tranquil Abiding very well or very long, even if we sit in the proper position and breathe the proper breaths. It's going to take time, but if you're gentle and consistent in training that puppy of a mind, you'll see progress. At the beginning, most of my students were very discouraged, and thought they were getting nowhere. And as you remember, I gave up altogether myself at one point, thinking the same thing.

But after a few months, most of them reported that friends, relatives, and coworkers were asking them what they were doing differently. They'd changed for the better, and people had noticed. Similar results emerged from the Shamatha* Project's measurements of the brains and bodies of novice meditators in a three-month Buddhist retreat. Most meditation classes are proving grounds. After so many millennia, there must be a reason why people in Asia are still spending so much time doing it, and why many of us in the West have taken it up.

---

* Their spelling of Shamata.

After two or three months in my weekly seminar, one student's sister suddenly died. Everyone at the funeral was grief-stricken. After she returned, the student told me, "Of course I was very sad, and will miss my sister very much. But I now had a way to work with my mind around the loss. I looked at the suffering people around me and thought, 'How are THEY going to deal with this?' I don't know how *I* could've dealt with it before doing this practice."

Rinpoche had to assure me again and again that it is fine to have thoughts arise. *Just so long as we don't grasp at or follow after them.* He gave the analogy of a still pond, perfectly reflecting the sky. Clouds will pass by from time to time, reflected in the pond. Then they pass on, and the pond is once again reflecting blue sky. Then another cloud and another, and so on. The pond doesn't leave its place to go chasing after this or that cloud. Our mind can be like that pond.

One metaphor I've come up with over the years is a rope passing across my open hand. I can either grab hold of the rope and get pulled off my seat, or I can let it pass through, registering the simple image and feeling of the rope as it passes but having no particular dramas around it, no need to grab on to it. Once it passes on, no feeling of the rope.

Over time I became more and more able to let the thoughts pass through. Whenever I noticed that I had been chasing a train of thought, I was able to make a *decision* to let it go, saying, "I don't have to think about that right now." What a relief! I really liked the open, buoyant feeling of not having to pursue a thought, of taking a vacation *in that very moment.* After some time, I developed that habit strongly enough that I am now able to do the same thing during the course of the day, in the moment.

> "Though the view should be as vast as the sky, keep your conduct as fine as barley flour."
> *Guru Rinpoche*

As Guru Rinpoche tells us, "Though the view should be as vast as the sky, keep your conduct as fine as barley flour."

People think meditation happens by the minute or hour, but it happens moment by moment.

Unrealistic Expectations
(OR, I WANT PATIENCE, AND I WANT IT NOW!)

As I've said, we can't have ridiculous, unrealistic expectations. If a teacher yells at a child when they do something they've always done before, the teacher is not going to have a very good student. It will actually take much longer to train that child, if at all, and both teacher and student will be absolutely miserable in the process.

Because the unconscious mind is much bigger and stronger than the conscious mind, I don't see how you can ever beat it into submission by saying, "Oh, I'm a lousy meditator. Look, I screwed up AGAIN!" Anyone who's ever tried to diet knows you can't bully the subconscious. It will win in the end. I've given up dieting and started really listening to what (and how much) my body actually wants. I've weighed about twenty pounds less for decades since.

Maybe our problem is that we think we should already be able to do this Shamata thing. It reminds me of my son: a week before his first piano lesson he urgently asked me to teach him some piano. I said, "But you're just about to start taking lessons." After increasingly insistent requests and my same answer, he finally replied, "But that's WHY I need you to teach me—quick, before I have to play at that first lesson!" He thought he already had to know how to play piano. I assured him that the teacher was expecting him to know nothing and was fully prepared to start teaching him from the beginning. So allow yourself to be a rank beginner! Even if you've tried this before, you might as well allow yourself to have the wandering mind of a sentient being. (I'll bet you still are one.) These practices are *designed* to start where we are and go from there.

Another problem is that while we're yelling at ourselves, we're definitely not doing Tranquil Abiding! The key to enlightenment is going beyond ego identification. But in the process of bawling ourselves out, we're producing a very dramatic movie in our minds . . . with ourselves as the star. This is the opposite of the object of the exercise.

As Westerners, and this is perhaps particularly true for Americans, we focus on the individual: self-sufficiency, self-reliance, individual rights, rugged individualism. These are all powerful and often positive and constructive concepts.

But if we focus only on our individual selves, we are also cultivating isolation, detachment, and a profoundly limited sense of the fundamental unity of all reality. A good medicine for this self-limiting loneliness would be to cultivate a new habit of being every time you sit down to meditate. You drop the drama that you're the star of (and—dare I mention it?—the *author*). You take a break from chasing after what you "need" and running from what is "bad" for you. You expand your definition of "I" (ego) to include all and everything, at least for a little while.

When We Realize We've Been Following a Thought

As noted, many modern people mentally beat themselves up just for *having* a train of thought and become so frustrated, and discouraged, that they can't sustain a full session of Tranquil Abiding.

In fact, Rinpoche *recommended* that I do meditation in mini sessions, meaning from moment to moment. No, not getting up and fixing breakfast! When we notice that we've been following a train of thought, at that moment—in that mini session—we're more aware than we've been for most of our life! Maybe many lives. That moment of noticing the movie is something to celebrate! If we praise the puppy whenever it does what we want, it will tend to do it more and more. Great! (One of the most useful insights of behavioral psychology, particularly the strand pioneered by B. F. Skinner, is that it is productive to reward the behavior we're looking for, but it is *not* productive to punish unwanted behavior, which should, instead, just be ignored.)

The moment we recognize we've been following a thought and we let it go—the moment of remembering (until we forget, and start making another movie)—marks the end of this mini session I'm speaking of. Then we settle back into that calm, bright, whole-ocean state. This marks the beginning of the next mini session.

We can do many of these mini sessions in one sitting (and, over time, they will get less "mini" as we do this practice). As a matter of fact, if we've done a lot of these, we've had a lot of moments of mindfulness, which is a great thing! So the arising of thoughts is actually an opportunity—grist for the mill of awakening.

In that moment when we've *realized* "Oh, I've just been following a train of thought," we have a great *opportunity*. We can choose to take a vacation from that drama and rest in buoyant, simple awareness. In

that instant we're really doing Tranquil Abiding. We probably can't stay in that state for more than a few moments, in the beginning, but that's okay. Contrary to popular belief, it's not how *long* we stay in that state, but how *often*, particularly in the beginning. Actually, Rinpoche has said that the more often we drop freshly into that state, the more we're having that alive, true experience. There is little chance for stagnation if we're constantly renewing that state.

The Tibetan word for meditate, *gom*, means a few different things. Depending on the spelling it can mean "meditate," "visualize," or "completely familiarize." The connotation of the last meaning is that we step onto this place with the familiarity of having experienced it again and again so that we have utter confidence. What a concept!

People sometimes think that if they have a moment of revelation or clarity, they've arrived. But have they really? Have they done more than take a peek? If they're still bumbling around, sowing seeds of disaster just as before, despite that revelatory experience, I'd say they might want to spend some *time* there—not just pass through on a single visit or two, and then talk about it, but take up residence there. It's the difference between taking a two-hour tour of Paris and moving there to live; you're not a Parisian just because you saw the Eiffel Tower from a tour bus. Enlightenment is a long, transformational process. The glimpses are crucial, but they're not the end, or the whole.

One time at a presentation by a panel of leaders from various faiths, a woman from the audience said that she'd had a near-death experience and since then had acquired clairvoyance and other amazing abilities. She'd been told that she was enlightened and was wondering if it was true. One panelist after another squirmed, danced around the question, and said a lot of nothing. The last panelist was Chagdüd Tulku, a Tibetan lama. He asked her three simple questions: "Do you ever feel lazy?" "Yes." "Do you ever feel desire or longing?" "Sure." "Do you ever feel angry?" "Well, yeah." "Then you're not enlightened."

Agitation: Perhaps Our Most Popular Pitfall
At least in the West, it seems.

The mind often falls into one of two states: agitation or dullness—mind racing around or else sunk in a stupor. Neither feels very good, and neither is what we're looking for here. Particularly in modern times—when we race around in planes, trains, and automobiles, and we work on computers that measure time in nanoseconds, and we watch images flash by on TV screens—our minds are all too often in a state of agitation, especially as we try to "multitask," as though it were an achievement to be doing more and more things simultaneously with less and less sustained and deep attentiveness. We dash from thought to thought, quite often getting nowhere fast (like the old joke: "We're lost, but we're making good time!"). I love the title of a book on meditation retreats: *Don't Just Do Something, Sit There*, by Sylvia Boorstein.

What do we do if we find ourselves in such an agitated state? Much of the above advice and insight help you to understand and deal with it. We can also rest our gaze a bit farther down; gaze at the lower part of the buddha in front of you. Yet another time-honored technique that sometimes helps is to put on an extra layer of clothing; the thought is that bodily warmth tends to slow the mind down.

BOREDOM AND OTHER CONCERNS: SOME SUGGESTIONS

STUDENT   *What about boredom?*

LT   I asked Rinpoche about that one too. Guess why. He said that boredom is a type of agitation, and that seen from another angle, it's simply another thought. Treat it like any thought. Touché. So in case he didn't already know it, I'd confirmed the fact that agitation is my personal favorite of the two pitfalls.

Chögyam Trungpa Rinpoche, who started the huge Shambhala *Sangha*, said that we Westerners needed to learn to experience *lots* of boredom. I believe he felt we needed to go through and out the other side of boredom, to acceptance of the boredom, until finally arriving at a quiet, spacious state. Remember that boredom, like amusement or stress or confusion, is in *us*, not in the situation—there's no such thing as a "boring situation," only a situation in which *we* are bored.

A common practice to help with this is to change the focus of your gaze. For example, if you've been looking at the whole figure, focus now on one particular part after another. If you've been doing that for a while, switch to the whole figure. This also keeps your eyes from getting overstrained. I've found this technique a helpful treatment for dullness too.

Sylvia Boorstein speaks of an experience she had with a Theravada technique of "mental noting," which helped her to keep bringing fresh awareness and presence to *each moment*, being ever present in the continual NOW, the "flow of awareness," as it's sometimes called. When she got the hang of it, she had this to say:

> A moment of mindfulness can feel ecstatic. I remember being amazed when I first began to discover the difference between talking about an experience and *being* the experience. The discovery of the rapture of mindfulness blew me away. Walking in a careful way, very present, I thought, "Talk about bizarre. *This* is bizarre: I'm totally putting my foot down." Putting a

foot down is not normally the sort of thing we think of as thrilling. But it *is* thrilling. It's not the foot that is thrilling. Mindfulness is thrilling.

STUDENT *I've just started doing Tranquil Abiding, and I find that my mind is even* MORE *busy than usual! I thought this practice was about resting the mind. Mine is just roaring along. Is there something wrong with me? Am I really going to be able to do this?*

LT This is such a common experience for people new to this practice that the ancient texts talked about it and gave it a name. As we spend time with this method, we go through successive stages of experience. The first one is referred to as a "waterfall." Now you know why! Actually our minds are very busy, with loud internal conversations all the time, but with our lens turned outward all the time, or caught up in the train of thought, we've never uncoupled ourselves from the drama and *observed* that fact before.

Congratulations! This is your first step in bringing mindfulness! I'm not kidding. It's a HUGE step, to finally really see what our minds are doing all the time. Without that step, the others can't follow. If you continue gently working with your mind as I've suggested here, that waterfall will become like a river of thoughts, then a slower one, and so on, until your mind becomes a vast, peaceful ocean. After a month or two you should notice a real difference, anyway—hopefully, in even less than a month. Not bad, after countless lifetimes of the waterfall!

STUDENT *I don't know if this falls into the agitation category, but whenever I try to do this practice, a great sadness overwhelms me. All I do is cry. This doesn't sound like the experience we're going for, and I wonder how helpful it is for me.*

LT Your experience is rare, but it does happen for some people. As we turn the lens from the compelling distraction of outer events, all of us sometimes experience a bubbling up of something sad, and a welling up of tears. Generally, meditation practice is the very best medicine to help us to move through and out the other side.

If this is your *consistent* experience *over time*, I would suggest not "gutting it out." In that case it tends not to get better as you go, and it could actually be detrimental for you. My suspicion is that some time spent in the right kind of psychotherapy would help. In extreme cases where we're suffering from post-traumatic stress disorder (PTSD), I recommend body-centered PTSD techniques in addition to meditation. Some psychotherapists already include both. Body-centered trauma work such as Hakomi or Bodynamics might be the best for some people. This approach would work not so much with words, but more directly on the nervous system and body itself, to clear away this obstacle.

Once you've cleared a good chunk of that, you might try Tranquil Abiding again. Meanwhile, you could try the other practices and see how they work for you.

Dullness, the Other Pitfall

We've spoken about the pitfall of agitation; now let's explore the other common one: dullness. Rinpoche has likened those repeated moments of awareness we were talking about to a mountain stream cascading over rocks and breaking up into tiny droplets, freshening the water.

He contrasted this stream with a stagnant pond. The water is swampy because it's just sitting there. If *we* just sit there in a stupor, we're not "familiarizing" (*gom*) with the state we want to cultivate. As we all know, stupor is not our natural state; it's one of the Three Poisons that obscures it.

Rinpoche often tells the story of a lama and his attendant in Tibet, traveling to Lhasa, the capital. They stopped along the way, where there was a stream below, so they could make tea. The attendant, who was a practitioner, climbed down with the teapot. As he was about to fill it, he looked over his shoulder and saw a tiny cave in the rock wall. He thought, "What a *perfect* little place to meditate!" He left the teapot by the water and settled down for a good session. As happens in some cases, he fell into a deep, unconscious state much like hibernation.

Time passed and the lama started to worry. He climbed down to the water himself, saw the teapot, but no attendant. He thought some animal must have carried his attendant off and eaten him! What could he do? He continued on to Lhasa by himself and stayed for nearly a year. When it was time to come home, he took the same road. As it happened, he stopped at the same place and climbed down to the stream with his teapot. (I guess it *was* a good stopping place.) It seems that the noise roused his attendant from his state of hibernation. The attendant called from the cave, "Are you ready for your tea?" He had no idea that a year had passed!

This is not an experience that a fellow should brag about to his friends. Rinpoche tells this story as a cautionary tale. Remaining in that blank state for a year, the young student was no closer to enlightenment, but he had lost a year of his life. Just stopping the mind is like pushing the pause button on your video player. The minute you push play again, you're right where you left off.

Many people sit in a vacuous state every day for years, thinking they're great meditators. Some of them proudly say that, even though the rest of their life is pretty miserable, while they're meditating they're feeling no pain. I feel great sadness when I think of that, and I hope they find better guidance. Really good guidance in the subtleties of mind training is all too rare.

STUDENT   *I find myself falling asleep sometimes. What should I do?*

LT   Whenever you feel dullness, even if you're not actually falling asleep, you can lift your gaze a little bit. If you're using a visual support, gaze at the figure's forehead, shoulders, topknot, etc. I also find it really helpful to take a big breath or two, to bring in fresh oxygen and generally clean out the cobwebs. It often helps to wear thinner clothing or cool off the room a bit. There are other helpful methods, such as prostrations, which you can learn later if you continue on this path. But for now you have a few tools in your kit.

STUDENT   *How long should I practice?*

LT   I REALLY don't mean to be glib, but for as long as you can without your puppy-dog mind resenting it or your monkey mind hijacking it. This varies wildly, from person to person, from day to day, from year to year. If you're a beginner, I would honestly recommend starting at FIVE MINUTES. Surprising, isn't it? But remember how briefly we have a puppy do its first "down-stay." Hopefully you'll give a five-minute Tranquil Abiding session your best attention. Then you can very gradually expand the number of minutes: next week, six minutes, etc.

Very soon you'll be alternating Tranquil Abiding with the next practice I'm about to introduce. Alternating the two keeps the practice fresh, alive, and focused. Your puppy-dog mind will thank you. With the two complementary practices, the session becomes more balanced and rich. The time seems to pass more quickly and easily too.

Yet Another Pitfall: Great Experiences

If I have a great experience of bliss, clarity, or non-thought . . . what's not to like? Well, *maybe* nothing; it depends on what you do with it. If you take it as an encouraging sign that you're on track, and then just keep going, no problem. In the case of Shamata in particular, and meditation practice in general, we tend to have experiences of bliss, clarity, and freedom from thoughts, from time to time. These can be quite lovely—intoxicating, even. It would be natural to want to go back to that state again and again. That would make it a pitfall; now you're feeling desire/clinging. As we've discussed, that usually leads us more *into* Samsara, not out of it. You're trying to get the meditation to go in a very particular way. Then, too, you're trying to repeat an experience from the past, so even if you could, you're preventing what you could experience *now.*

Another response would be to feel proud about your achievement, letting it drop in conversations with people, or maybe making up a story in your mind about how you'll be as a meditation teacher, now that you've come so far. As you may have guessed by now, that would be another way of going into ego identification and Samsara instead of away from it.

When you do have a positive meditation experience—called *nyam* in Tibetan—it's all right to celebrate for a moment. You just came to an encouraging signpost—good work!

Then, as with any other thought or appearance, let go of it. After all, if you're walking down a road and come to a signpost letting you know you're where you were hoping to be, do you feel all proud? Do you sit down by the post and refuse to move? You just quickly register, "Good, I'm on the right road," and continue on. If you let go of that nyam too, then you're open to all of the other experiences that you may have, further down the road . . . including, eventually, enlightenment.

Beginning the Session

Before you begin the session, set a planned amount of time and stick to it. If you end early, you'll quickly develop that habit and it will be VERY hard to change. This is another reason it's good to start with a relatively short time, so you'll be able to meet the plan you set for yourself. Deciding on an amount of time and actually doing the session that long gives you personal power and lets you build momentum to do it more easily the next time. Habits, habits.

Many people set a timer. There's even a company that sells clocks that count down whatever time you set, then ring a lovely little Zen-style chime. The company is called Now and Zen. Cute. Another company, Enso, sells one called Pearl. It's more compact, which is nice, but it doesn't have a real chime. Now there are better and better alarm/alert phone apps that you could probably use as well. Just be sure your calls don't come through!

If, realistically, you have only fifteen minutes, then set your time for fifteen, including the Clearing of the Stale Energies, dedication prayers, and so on. I did that for years, and it was easy to stick to. As I felt the benefits, I naturally wanted to make the time longer. As my mind got used to the "getting used to" (my looser translation of *gom*), I could go to twenty, thirty, and eventually ninety minutes, and even two hours. In retreat I've done MANY sessions for three hours. In the beginning I never would have guessed that I'd end up being *able* to do that, much less enjoy it! Even if you never reach that length, you'll reap plenty of benefit from twenty or thirty minutes for your daily sessions. I'm not telling you this from blind faith or the exceptional experience; I'm telling you this after hearing it from dozens and dozens of students.

Ending the Session

Once you've come to the end of your session, you want to conclude it by once again remembering that you're making this effort on behalf of all beings, not just yourself. Remember: we're always trying to come from the view of the whole ocean—not just "me, the wave." So you do the other end of the "bodhicitta bookends" that bracket your session.

Because all beings are also stuck in this predicament called Samsara, we want to end with prayers for their eventual freedom, along with our own—once again, the Two Purposes. I've included a couple of traditional Tibetan prayers for you to say at this point. I've offered the first one in both English (because of course you need the meaning) and Tibetan (because some of you might want to use the same sounds that many others have used for so many years). The sounds themselves do carry power, and that's worth something too. The chanted Tibetan has a rhythm to it which is sweet and compelling. If you ever find yourself with Tibetans, they'll most likely know one or two of these prayers, so you'll be able to "sing along." Then, too, I've noticed that some Westerners just get a kick out of Tibetan clothes, sounds, prayer flags, and so on. So for all those reasons I thought I'd include the Tibetan too.

This first prayer is for Ngöndro, the set of Preliminary Practices. Despite the name, you would actually do these practices after already making some progress with the ones in this book (but you can do the prayer anytime). There is a dedication/aspirational prayer at the end of the session, which kind of says it all, in my mind. But an added benefit is that if you decide to do the Preliminary Practices, you'll already know the ending prayer. Here it is, along with another one:

DEDICATION OF MERIT

Gewa di yi nyur du dak Orgyen Lama drup gyur ne
By this virtue may I swiftly *Attain the state of the Lama of Orgyen,**

Drowa jik kyang ma lü pa De yi sa la gö par shok
And bring all beings without exception *To that level.*

or:

By the power of this compassionate practice,
May suffering be transformed into peace.
May the hearts of all beings be open,
And their wisdom radiate from within.**

If you already have a Root Lama, you would conclude with his or her long-life prayer.

In Conclusion

So take your meditation a moment at a time. Each time you actually realize you're following after thoughts, *rejoice* at your realization . . . and drop back into resting your eyes on the image, and resting your mind in fresh, alive, joyful awareness. And that next moment of pure Tranquil Abiding will pass too, but that's okay. You'll have another fresh one. Many per session, I hope!

Now that's real freedom!

Over time, I became able to take a vacation in the middle of daily life, in just the same way as I do in those moments of awareness. "Oh, I don't have to follow that." *Now that's real freedom!*

---

* One of the many epithets for Guru Rinpoche, who of course reached full enlightenment.
** Originally composed in English. Used by the Tergar Sangha, led by Mingyur Rinpoche.

I'll say it again: *That's real freedom.* Having to follow after your thoughts like a dog on a leash isn't. It's slavery, just like my having to buy and smoke cigarettes back when I was a smoker was also slavery. When our mind plays a painful scene over and over, sometimes we can't seem to stop it. But replaying it is like picking at a wound so that it can never heal. If someone hits you with a tennis racket, that person did it once and moved on. But if you play the scene over and over again, it's like you've picked up the racket and continued the beating. You've just beaten yourself a hundred times. Yet we can't always stop ourselves through force of will. Therefore, training is needed.

Not only was it a relief to be freer of such things, but it kept me from compulsively following a neurosis-driven train of thought that would have led to unfortunate speech and/or action, planting karmic seeds, sending me on another turn of the wheel. Needless to say, it wouldn't have helped the other person involved either. How many of us have *known* we should leave a situation or a nasty remark well enough alone . . . and *can't*? Of course, I still find myself wishing I'd left well enough alone many times on any and all of the above. Practice, practice.

FURTHER STUDY

I've given you a very quick introduction to Tranquil Abiding, or Shamata. If you find you really want to do this practice regularly, there are many sources that go into it much more fully. The best two I know of are very different and complement each other well.

The first is a meditation kit by Joseph Goldstein and Sharon Salzberg. They studied this method with great masters in Burma and Thailand for years, then studied, practiced, and taught it in America for decades. They're genuine masters in their own right, and make it all very accessible—a winning combination! You can buy their kit at Sounds True or at many Dharma bookstores. Ours, for example.

My one caveat is that their version of this method was learned from the Theravada Lineage, so it differs in some ways from the particular version I've just laid out for you. For example, they don't specify to breathe through the mouth, but in my particular lineage, we do. They insist that you remain motionless during the sitting portion (they alternate this practice with Walking Meditation); we don't. There are other differences too. If you take one of their retreats, you're free to decide what variations you want to do, except that of course if they specify something like Walking Meditation, you'll probably want to go with the program. But they won't object if you keep your eyes open, for example.

Another difference with the Insight Meditation Society, where Goldstein and Salzberg teach, is that though they begin with Shamata, they very quickly introduce Vipassana, or Insight Meditation, which is a partner to Shamata. In Rinpoche's style of teaching, he brings in other practices before Vipassana, and generally doesn't emphasize either Shamata or Vipassana nearly as much. Unlike the Insight Meditation Society, he doesn't see them as an end in themselves.

The Shamata I've taught here is designed to prepare you for a succession of Vajrayana practices. If you intend to go on to other Vajrayana practices—particularly the ones in our lineage—you'll naturally want to do Tranquil Abiding more like the variation in this book and work in the other practices rather than going immediately to Vipassana and emphasizing it.

I also strongly recommend a book on this topic by my lama, Tulku Sangak Rinpoche. (Please see Appendix C, Recommended Reading, for more info.) It's a nice balance to the book you're now reading as well as the kit I just mentioned, in that it gives lots of background and instruction that I don't include here. I've given you a bit of introduction and context that I think is essential for Westerners, because that's what I can do as a Westerner. And unlike the Insight Meditation Society folks, I'm a Vajrayana (Tibetan Buddhist) practitioner.

SCIENCE TIDBIT

My Own Little Experiment

A few years ago, I had the chance to use a biofeedback device that measured the coordination, or "coherence" (as HeartMath, the creators of the device, called it), between my brain and my heart. (For a fuller explanation, see www.heartmath.org.) Normally it takes training to coordinate them much at all. When we have negative emotions, for example, the line on the readout graph looks squiggly, random, and, well, incoherent. When there's 100 percent coherence, it shows a perfect sine wave—perfectly round hills and valleys.

When I was first hooked up to the device, the graph readout showed a sloppy sine wave. There were hills and valleys, but rough. Then the coach asked me to imagine a bear chasing me. At the moment I clearly visualized and felt the experience in my mind, the biofeedback readout suddenly went completely haphazard. It looked like the track of an insane bug.

Then he asked me to think of something inspiring.

I immediately knew what to choose: my favorite part of my meditation sessions—why not? In that part, my Root Lama, Rinpoche, appears as Guru Rinpoche, the enlightened master who transformed Tibet into a Buddhist country. The image is colorful, beautiful, and inspiring. And for me it's enlivened by my feeling the presence of my own master, Rinpoche. I closed my eyes and recited the beautiful little prayer that goes with it, imagining Rinpoche slowly coming down into my heart. Then we mingled together into one awareness. I rested there.

When I opened my eyes, the readout showed a perfect sine wave. The biofeedback technician was shocked. Normally, after working with the device for weeks, people can get a reasonably coherent sine wave, indicating coherence between the brain and heart. I had immediately gone to 100 percent coherence and stayed there the entire time. Of course, as soon as I stopped the visualization, the readout showed a sloppy sine wave like the one in the beginning. I still needed to do more practice!

When I tried this again later, with other Buddhist practices, I had exactly the same results. When I opened my eyes, I was jubilant, saying, "Hey, this shit works!" (Whereupon, the sine wave immediately got sloppy again.) But since I'd already experienced my own inner transformation and gotten feedback from many other people, why was I surprised? Why did I need a machine to validate what I already knew? Still, for some reason I thought you might like to hear about this.

Rinpoche is Tibetan, and, though he doesn't even speak English (of course he had the book translated), his book will give you further context in a very different way, and bring you a level of depth and understanding—both intellectually and experientially—that only he can offer.

One other master who is both a Westerner and a Vajrayana teacher is Pema Chödrön. You can find books and recordings of her teaching Shamata.

If you really want to check into this practice, you'll make it easier for yourself if you just *go do* a Shamata retreat. Nothing can replace having live teachings from a qualified teacher, and then having the optimal container—retreat—in which to road test the teachings.

One teacher, Anam Thubten Rinpoche, who does this quite well is Tibetan, but his English is better than many Americans'. He especially enjoys using colloquial turns of phrase, to the delight of his listeners. He really gets the point across too.

Ewam and Namchak are two 501(c)(3) charters under our one Sangha, led by Tulku Sangak Rinpoche. If you would like to try one of our Shamata retreats, you can look at our schedule at Namchak.org. The website for Ewam International is Ewam.org.

TONGLEN

Tranquil Abiding helps us calm the waters of the mind, allowing us to experience truth more clearly. We can learn a lot through studying the nature of the mind and reality, but we can't stop there.

Tranquil Abiding helps us to *see* for *ourselves*, through stilling the mind and experiencing insight. Through connecting with *others*, as a compassionate act, Tonglen helps us *feel* how we're not separate from the rest of the ocean.

This balance is important. The Tibetan scriptures speak of many pairs. In *Why Bother?* I mentioned their definition of enlightenment: cleansing our obscurations (the windshield) and fully maturing our buddha qualities (evidence of our Buddha Nature.) Tranquil Abiding helps with the former; Tonglen with the latter. Another pair is wisdom (Tranquil Abiding) and compassion (Tonglen).

I've said that Vajrayana (Tibetan Buddhism) meets us where we are, and supports us in our journey from there. So it is with Tonglen. From time to time, we will all imagine someone and have an imagined interaction with them. Well, here, you get to do that as an official part of the exercise! We also tend to feel great compassion for those we're close to in our lives, and not so much for others. We get to start with that tendency, then expand from there.

I'll get to the specifics in a bit, but first I want to tell you a little more about Tonglen in general. As you progress along this path, you'll see that we're often given methods that alternate between purifying our karmic windshield and expanding our buddha qualities—again, the Tibetan understanding of cleansing away impurities and maturing our Buddha Nature, *sang-gye*. As Rinpoche has said, wisdom without compassion can lead to the creation of atom bombs. Compassion without wisdom is ineffectual, and can just be a nice sentiment. We don't want to develop one while ignoring the other. Now that you've started cleaning your windshield, here's a practice that expands your capacity for compassion.

Tonglen is a Tibetan form of compassion practice that's used in different forms in all of the lineages of the Dharma. Within Vajrayana (Tibetan Buddhism) there are many sub-branch lineages, all of which practice Tonglen, but as with many of the practices, they vary a bit, from one to another. The word *Tonglen* means "sending and receiving" in Tibetan. In this practice, we basically imagine breathing in the suffering of others and breathing out our wish for them to be happy.

The Setup

Before beginning the practice, I often bring to mind some kind of suffering I'm experiencing in my own life at the moment. Since my life is rarely perfect, I can usually find a juicy subject for my practice. Sometimes I've heard of another person who's suffering terribly, so I naturally focus on that. Then, too, if I hear of a natural disaster or war that destroyed many lives, it's natural for me to focus on those people and animals. Wherever my passion is, that's a likely place for me to start the practice of *com*passion.

For the moment, let's say you've picked your own suffering. Let's say it's the feeling that your life is meaningless, and, naturally, you're upset about that. You've got a job that's meaningless; when you go home, there's not much meaning going on. You feel powerless to change your life, and you're coming ever closer to the end of it without hope of doing more meaningful work or having more meaningful relationships. I believe this is what Thoreau was referring to when he spoke of most people leading lives of "quiet desperation." In this situation, you may start with doing Tonglen for yourself, or you may take that strong feeling and begin practicing for someone you care about who is enduring a similar kind of suffering: a dearth of meaning in their life.

If another kind of suffering (yours or someone else's) is more immediate, though, such as loneliness, grief, guilt, or frustration, then go ahead and pick that. In other words, choose whatever feels most acute and important to you as you prepare to begin.

Tibetans traditionally begin by imagining someone they feel natural sympathy for who has a particular kind of suffering. Many of us in the West have found it really helpful to start with ourselves, an approach which may sound narrowly egotistical, but isn't necessarily. Since most of us haven't got enough compassion for *ourselves*, what basis do we have for expanding that toward others? The Golden Rule, "Do unto others as you would have them do unto you," doesn't work if we don't have compassion for ourselves. It's the same with "Love thy neighbor as thyself." Because we Westerners tend to *think about* painful circumstances (our own, or others') rather than fully and feelingly experience them, we often do Tonglen more as an intellectual exercise than as a (com)passionate act. This practice is intended to strongly engage our emotion—the *positive* emotion of compassion.

So the two decisions to make before you start are (1) which "theme" you're working with and (2) whether you'll start with yourself or another.

The Actual Practice

GETTING STARTED

Sit with your back relatively straight so your yeshe winds are likely to be stronger. The Tibetans say, "When the spine is straight, the channels are straight. When the channels are straight, the winds go straight. When the winds go straight, the mind goes straight." After having done the Tibetan Nose Blow, you are no doubt coming to understand how this works.

Bring to mind the subject of suffering you've chosen. Again, I recommend that you generally start the session by doing Tonglen for yourself. You then go the next rung out: sending and receiving for someone else—someone you easily feel strong compassion for—who is experiencing the same kind of suffering you have in your life right now. For example, if I'm suffering from my own grief, and I bring to mind a Tibetan friend I know whose father and brothers were all suddenly taken away and never heard from again, I can REALLY feel for her.

THE CORE

As you begin this practice, I'm assuming you've just finished doing Shamata, but if not, first flash on that ultimate ocean of awareness. It has many qualities—such as vastness, absolute power (to create everything), and absolute compassion. This Absolute, or Ultimate, Bodhicitta comes from the awakened mind of Absolute Truth. So "change channels" and bring your mind to that Absolute Bodhicitta level for just a moment as a starting point for this practice.

Now, clearly imagine someone in front of you, someone you easily feel sympathetic to—as we discussed, it could be yourself. Even if the eventual focus of your practice is someone else, I highly recommend you *precede* this by imagining yourself, in your own suffering. Place your small, suffering self in your heart, or out in front—experiment with what works best for you. Only then should you proceed to do Tonglen, first for yourself, then for your suffering friend, etc., in ever-widening circles. If you've chosen victims of a natural disaster or war or catastrophe, then go ahead and start with them. I'd recommend imagining them as individuals, one by one, to start with, so it's more immediate and intimate. See each face in pain.

Perhaps you've already brought your own loneliness up and are feeling the pain of that. Now you open yourself up to the pain of your friend. Now you're *really* feeling compassion! Of *course* you want to take away their suffering. Now's your chance!

In this movie you're doing, you breathe in their suffering in the form of dark clouds, coming from them right into your heart. Yes, you breathe it into your heart, where you feel your compassion for them, the part that passionately doesn't want them to suffer, the part that wants to take their suffering away. This is com*passion* at work. At this point, I quite often have tears.

In this next part of your movie (sometimes it's *good* to make movies in your mind!), you breathe out your wish for them to be happy. This wish appears as white, sparkling clouds, going from your heart to them. It surrounds and soaks into them.

If they're suffering from a useless life, now you imagine them doing what they'd REALLY love to do, something that fills their hearts with satisfaction. They're smiling.

If the suffering is loneliness, we imagine them basking in love. Their face is transformed into a huge smile. They're glowing. We find ourselves smiling too. We want them to be *completely* free from suffering and happy *always*.

Let yourself really *feel* all this. By now, I often find that my eyes still have tears and my mouth now has a smile.

Breathe in the suffering again. You probably didn't take it all away in the first breath, and you don't want to leave any suffering, or skimp on giving them joy. You want them *100 percent, permanently happy*! Why not eternal bliss?! Send out the joy to them again, on the sparkling clouds of your breath, imagining that now they're completely enlightened and will remain eternally joyful.

As you do this a few times you, too, might notice tears in your eyes and a smile on your face, all at the same time. It's not required, but it sometimes happens that way. We feel the suffering as we breathe in, AND we feel satisfaction and joy as we *finally* have a chance to *do* something about it.

But let's not stop there. That's only one person. Now do the same operation for someone else whom you can easily feel compassion for, who has (or has had) a similar kind of suffering. Do a few breaths for them. Now another, then another. People—maybe animals too—are starting to pop up all around you.

Now you're ready to move to the next rung out. In this rung of con-centric circles, you imagine people (or creatures) you don't have such strong affinity for, perhaps distant acquaintances or people you've heard about in passing. Maybe they have a similar kind of suffering. Now that we've gotten a tide of compassion going in ourselves, we can feel just about as passionate about also ridding them of suffering. Now that we think of it, we want *them* to be happy too. Ultimate, everlasting joy—sure! So we breathe for them.

For the next rung out, imagine whole *classes* of creatures: waifs on the streets of Mexico City, slaves, drug addicts, bullied kids, people dying of cancer, whatever goes with your theme. Riding on the strong waves of passionate compassion, we strongly want to take away their misery too, and make them happy. We breathe for them.

After you've done this practice for a few weeks, you may want to really stretch your compassion muscles and do Tonglen for somebody you don't like, someone who's caused you trouble. They might even be a troublemaker or enemy. At this point in the practice, you might be able to see them simply as a misguided sentient being, trying to pursue happiness and ending up with suffering. (Sound like anybody you know? Everybody? Yourself, even?) Breathe for them.

At some time or another, EVERY being in Samsara, both seen and unseen, has certainly suffered similarly. They will in the future, too. Since linear time is another illusory appearance, we can breathe for ALL of them. That means absolutely everybody. Who would we want to leave out? So, last, breathe for them all.

Now rest for a bit. This is often a good time to do Shamata again.

DEDICATION AND ASPIRATIONS

Finish with the concluding prayers (see page 59). Then pause for a moment before rushing back into the fray of daily life. You've earned that moment of basking—why not take it?

Questions (and Answers!)

STUDENT *I'm a little nervous: if I do Tonglen for someone with cancer, will I get cancer?*

LT I must confess I had the same worry too, in the beginning. Only if you're a very highly realized being could that happen, in which case you'd also be able to transform their affliction. In either case, then, I don't see how you'd get sick. Let me use some really easy examples. If you did Tonglen for someone with a broken arm, would your arm break? If you did Tonglen for someone whose beloved dog had died, would yours suddenly die? You see my point?

STUDENT *Well, when you put it like that . . .*

STUDENT *I find I'm skittish about breathing in someone's problems. I really don't want to let that in. To be honest, I'm actually scared of the feeling.*

LT This brings us to a very important distinction: You're not breathing in their *story.* You're breathing in their *suffering.* Remember, too, that those dark clouds get transformed to bright ones with every breath. How? The next very important point: *through your strong feeling of compassion.* The transformation happens through the power of the desire in our heart for that person to be free of suffering and to be happy. It's kind of like photosynthesis: a plant "breathes" in carbon dioxide and "breathes" out oxygen; in Tonglen, we breathe in suffering and breathe out happiness.

The stronger your feeling of compassion, the less you have to worry about getting brought down by the dark cloud.

To put it another way, you won't get weighed down by the dark clouds of suffering if you want the person to be happy. Why? Since your very feeling of compassion wants to take away their suffering and make them happy, the visualization will naturally follow your mind, your intention, what you want to happen. The compassion is the catalyst.

Here's a key point: Remember to keep your breaths of equal length and intensity. Paltry breaths in, with big, strong breaths out, is anemic compassion. Then again, if you do intense in-breaths, really taking in the suffering, then puny out-breaths, you'll end up feeling depleted and depressed. So keep your breaths long, equal, and full, allowing your robust feelings of compassion to perform the alchemy.

STUDENT   *What if I come upon a car accident or I'm visiting a relative in the hospital? Can I do Tonglen right then and there?*

LT   Triage Tonglen is an excellent thing to do! We're inspired in the moment, and there seems to be some scientific proof that prayer really may help with healing, for example. Why leave it only for the meditation room? That doesn't mean we should give up doing the full practice as I've described, but in-the-moment Tonglen for someone suffering right in front of you is a great thing to do in addition. Besides, it could have a very real effect.

STUDENT *I tried doing it for my husband, whom I'm planning to divorce. When it came to the in-breath, I just really didn't want to take anything in. The same thing happened when I tried it with a politician I especially loathe. What should I do?*

LT Politicians? Your almost ex-husband? You're really going for extra credit! Seriously, you could do one of two things: (1) Remember that you're only taking in his *suffering*, not his personality, his politics, his bad vibes, or whatever it is that you really don't want to take in. As I mentioned before, you're seeing him as a misguided sentient being with suffering, and then breathing in the suffering itself. If you think of the karma that the politician or whoever is gathering for themselves, you can then imagine their next life and feel compassion. (2) You can just opt out of doing Tonglen for him at this point. There's no law that says you have to do Tonglen for him today—this year, even.

Many Tibetans were eventually able to have great, sincere compassion for the Chinese, even their torturers. When one monk who had been tortured and beaten countless times in his thirty-five years in prison was finally released and arrived in India, he had an audience with His Holiness the Dalai Lama. The Dalai Lama asked him what his greatest fear was during that whole, harrowing time. "My greatest fear was that I might lose compassion," he replied. But then he said that when he saw the great

unhappiness in his torturer's face, he found himself able to feel compassion for him. His fear was laid to rest.

STUDENT   *I'm embarrassed to say that I find my mind wandering off track from time to time.*

LT   Yeah, so does mine. You noticed that with Shamata too, no doubt. Here's a little secret I'll let you in on: EVERY practice, on one level, is about forgetting and remembering, forgetting and remembering. Slowly, slowly, we make progress. The point is that we're trying to be more mindful. We're not there yet, which is why we call all of these "practices." Please practice compassion for your wiggly-puppy mind. Practice compassion for yourself.

Additional Comments

Whenever I've been suffering from physical or mental pain, I almost always find that my lens has gotten very small. The pain fills the whole lens. This is just what I don't want, because then my experience is 100 percent suffering. How ironic. How human. This practice opens the lens *wide*. The pain is exactly the same, but it takes up a tiny fraction of my lens now. Even though this practice hasn't fixed my actual problem, it transforms the experience altogether. That's worth a lot!

Beyond that, the more we do this practice, the more we expand our capacity for compassion. You don't have to take my word. Many fMRI studies done at the University of Wisconsin–Madison and elsewhere have consistently measured brain activity, some in particular locations, and some at particular wave frequencies, that indicate high levels of compassion in longtime Buddhist meditators. We're talking, literally, off the charts! This was particularly true while they were meditating, but even in between sessions.

For more specifics on this, you could start by reading chapter 16 of *Happiness*, by Matthieu Ricard, or by visiting the website of the Mind and Life Institute. In addition to the studies, the institute lists books they've generated from the meetings they've held between scientists and the Dalai Lama. You might find a number of them interesting. Frankly, I find I'm like a kid in a candy store when I look at their book list!

As you may have guessed, Tonglen is a powerful practice, if done full-heartedly. It can be very healing. It can also be very challenging. Again, practice compassion on yourself, so you can be successful with this. Only you can judge how long your sessions should be. While you're still new to the practice, I'd recommend doing it for five minutes at a time, alternating it with Shamata. And, as with Shamata, you can lengthen your sessions as you become more familiar with the practice.

FURTHER READING ON TONGLEN

There's one book on this topic that I'd recommend—I'd say it's required reading if you're serious about doing Tonglen. It's a tiny little book, devoted entirely to this practice, titled *Tonglen, the Path of Transformation* (hope you can remember that title). The author is a nun in the Tibetan tradition, and an American by birth, Pema Chödrön. Her instructions are very similar to what we've covered, but she goes into some more areas there than I do here. Pema Chödrön's style is very human, direct, laser-like, yet utterly compassionate. She's offered many excellent books and recordings on Buddhist topics, and I've really appreciated every one of them I've experienced. You can find her offerings at Sounds True and Shambhala Publications.

Instructional audio for Tonglen is available at Namchak.org

DOING DAILY PRACTICE

Round Robin

I've thrown a lot at you, and when you sit down to practice, you might be just a wee bit confused. What do you do first? Then what? For how long? I've found for myself that the part of my mind that's doing practice is not the part that can go down a list. Besides, after the intensity of doing some Tonglen, for example, it's hard to remember where I'm at in the whole larger progression of the session. So later in this chapter I've provided you with a simple list you can look through right now. And I've created a practice card (in the back of the book) you can keep by your meditation spot. Then again, you could just bookmark that page. You can also write out a shorter version, once you're really used to it.

With our busy modern lives, I find that it's difficult to stick with one form of meditation for a long time. Besides, as you remember, Rinpoche recommends breaking up the sessions to keep our experience fresh, while at the same time keeping us on the cushion. Chagdüd Tulku also recommends alternating practices for short periods, and I've found this really effective, especially for beginners.

One Tibetan doctor noticed that many of the students at our center, like most of his Western patients, had too much of the air element (similar to the old Western medical model of the "humors"). He told all of them not to meditate consecutively for more than *five minutes*, because the restless air element couldn't handle it and they would only get more agitated. To address the problem, I recommended this Round Robin Meditation method of alternating practices every five minutes. Everyone who tried it found they could sit for twenty minutes without the ill effects the doctor had warned them about.

Since I've found most Americans respond well to this Round Robin method, I tend to think the doctor is onto something. I also like that the Round Robin has us changing gears all the time, keeping our practice fresh. Here, then, is a suggested procession of events for your sessions, which you can modify in some ways as you go. I've put it on the next page.

Sample Daily Practice Session
ROUND ROBIN MEDITATION

- **1 MINUTE OR LESS:** Check motivation for doing this practice in this session. Bring forward bodhicitta motivation (the Two Purposes) if necessary. (HINT: It almost always needs a little bringing forward, but don't expect it to be 100 percent before moving on—that's what the practice is *for*, after all.)

- **10 TO 15 SECONDS:** Offer three short prostrations. *Optional.* (Description on pages 83 to 84.)

- **1 MINUTE:** Clearing the Stale Energies. Rest.

- **5 MINUTES:** Shamata.

- **5 MINUTES:** Tonglen.

- **5 MINUTES:** Shamata.

  (*Optional:* If you have the time, you could alternate between Shamata and Tonglen again and again. It's good to end this part with at least a bit of Shamata before going to the concluding stage.)

- **30 SECONDS:** Dedication of merit and aspirational prayers.

  If you have a Root Lama, you would recite their long-life prayer at this time.

Guided meditation of this practice available at Namchak.org

The Practice of Doing Daily Practice

The easiest part about daily practice is actually doing it. In my years of practicing and teaching, I've seen that the hardest thing is *getting one's butt to the cushion on a daily basis.* In other words, *starting* is the hardest part. But of course, without starting, there's no practice at all. So here are some tips to help you with what is, for many, the most difficult practice: The Doing of Daily Practice.

First of all, I suggest that in the beginning you give yourself a really attainable goal: fifteen minutes a day. Trust me: thirty minutes every other day won't work as well. For one thing, every other day is a much harder rhythm to establish than every day. For another, we want to be compassionate with our minds and not make them try to do something so new for more than fifteen minutes a day, in the beginning. And a third reason: when you're learning a new language, it wouldn't work to do two hours on Saturday, and nothing the rest of the week. It's much better to do a little every day. The same is true for learning a musical instrument. This training is no different. And our minds, like our muscles, seem to "learn" to do more effectively what we do more regularly.

Yet another reason for starting with fifteen-minute sessions is that it's hard to come up with a believable excuse for not taking *fifteen minutes.* When we tell ourselves that we don't *have* time for something, it almost always means that we're choosing not to *take* time for something (fifteen minutes a day still leaves you twenty-three hours and forty-five minutes for other pursuits—and if your life's so hectic that you don't feel as though you can spare fifteen minutes, you really *do* need some Tranquil Abiding).

The last reason is that our whole purpose here is to change long-established habits of the mind. It's been proven that doing something daily is most effective at changing habits. The rule that I keep hearing again and again is that if you do something every day for twenty-one days, it becomes a habit. Alcoholics Anonymous uses this theory in their work.

I should probably repeat my personal favorite: I think of my daily practice as a vacation. We all need a vacation, but even when we take a trip to Hawaii, we take our busy minds with us. Doing practice can feel even better than sitting on a beach, stewing about the nasty thing so-and-so said to you. This is a *real* vacation, and I want to take it every day!

Okay, I have to confess that I hardly ever take an actual vacation, in the normal sense of the word. I'm kind of a workaholic (perhaps the apple doesn't fall far from the paternal tree?). So the motivator that usually actually gets me on the cushion is to say, "Since this will help all of your work go better, this is your most important work for the day." I once saw a refrigerator magnet that said something like, "When I don't meditate, I waste a lot more time running around like a chicken with its head cut off." The five years I didn't meditate proved these last two points to me, about efficiency and focus, beyond a doubt.

> This is a *real* vacation and I want to take it every day!

Working It Into Your Schedule

This is a key to success in your practice, so let's spend some time on this one. It's best, but not essential, to do your sessions just as you wake up in the morning. Most Tibetan practitioners do theirs at this time because the border between sleeping and waking provides an especially good opportunity to catch the mind at the beginning of the day, before it's fallen into its old ruts and gained momentum. We step into the day with a bit more mindfulness, and all the thousands of decisions that you make that day can be made from that state of mind. Then, too, early morning is usually a much quieter time, with a calm, clear feeling to it—none of the bustle of the rest of the day. The waters of the mind tend to be more settled, clear, and fresh . . . especially after Clearing the Stale Energies!

When I had small children at home, they were early risers, so I had trouble getting a good session in before they woke up. Tibetans often get up at incredibly early hours to make time for their sessions. Being a lazy American who needs something like a full night's sleep, I did the next best thing and meditated at night after the kids were asleep, and hopefully *before* I was (when I was on the *other* border between sleeping and waking).

Whatever time you've decided on, a key to success is *keeping to your sessions in the same part of your daily schedule.* I think that's why we succeed in brushing our teeth so regularly: the momentum of routine and habit is unbelievably strong. We've talked about how negative momentum can work against us, but we can use positive momentum

to work in our favor, once the good habit is established. If your bed-
time varies, that's less than optimal but still workable. Just as you can
brush your teeth a bit later because you're going to bed a bit later, you
can meditate a bit later too. If you can't do your session at exactly the
same time each day, just keep it in the same part of your routine.

   If you're doing your sessions at some place or time other than sitting up in bed first thing in the morning, begin by facing your shrine,
or at least a picture of a buddha and/or your Root Lama. If you're
going to offer three prostrations, this is when you would do them.

How to Do a Prostration

Before I describe *how*, I should probably mention to *whom/what* we prostrate. We prostrate to the Three Jewels: (1) the enlightened mind of the Buddha, (2) his teachings—the Dharma—which instruct us how to become enlightened ourselves, and (3) the Sangha, the congregation of like-minded people pursuing this path of enlightenment.

The Buddha saw all three of these as essential if we're to reach our goal of enlightenment. I'll say more about this a bit later. For now I'll say that, in addition to daily practice, it's a wonderful support to have others—Sangha—reading, studying, and practicing this same material with you. If you don't already have such friends at hand, please look at Appendix A for how you can find like-minded people nearby, and how to set up a weekly study/learning circle. Or you can find it all on our website: Namchak.org.

To put it *very* succinctly, prostrations are yet another way to loosen our ferocious grip on ego identification: lower mind bows to higher mind; small self to the larger Self.

We bow down on the floor. We literally get down on our knees and lower our heads to the ground. In a full prostration, we then stretch out, facedown. Then reverse the whole process to get up. Before and after each sequence, we put our hands together in prayer position, then touch the forehead, throat, and heart. When we do that at the end of one prostration, it serves as the beginning of the next.

I experience prostration as a kinesthetic reminder that, in right relationship, the lower self serves the greater Self. This action gets that thought literally *into our bones*. We touch the three places and bow down, paying homage to the greater Self with our body, speech, and mind. If you have a Root Lama, they hopefully have that meaning for you, so you offer the prostrations to them. In any case, you can use the picture of an enlightened being, such as the one included in the card packet in the back. Both the lama and the enlightened being represent the Three Jewels in this way: their body is the Sangha, their speech is the Dharma, and their mind is the Buddha. Now that you've reminded yourself in such a dramatic way of right relationship of self to Self, you're ready to begin your session.

Setting

As with other regular routines, we can really be supported by having a regular *place* to practice, with conditions that work in our favor.

So you'll need a place that's conducive to practice. As with practicing the piano, you don't go out and perform before you've practiced at home with no pressure or distractions. So it is with this kind of practice. The practices are designed to help you eventually apply your developing capacities in daily life, but we can hardly expect ourselves to do that right away. I wouldn't suggest performing a concert after your first piano lesson either.

Being isolated from outside demands will clearly help. I knew one practitioner who answered his phone while in "session"! His progress was disappointing, of course. So don't just turn your cell phone off—turn it off and put it in another room. The whole point is to give ourselves the chance not to respond to stimuli and distractions from the outside for a bit. Then we can turn the lens inward.

Another support I've already mentioned is a statue or picture of an enlightened being. Tibetans like to have statues and paintings of enlightened deities and great masters where they practice. They also keep relics there. Scientists have now confirmed that states of mind can be infectious. Tibetans already knew this, as well as the power of archetypal images. We might as well have that knowledge work for us.

If you create a special place or shrine that's just for meditation, that can really work well for you. Our brains work by association, and if we associate that place with meditation, we'll have even more momentum working for us. Time and again, students have reported their practice improving by leaps and bounds as soon as they set up a meditation spot for themselves.

Frame of Mind

If I gave you one piece of advice, from one Western practitioner to another, it would be this: practice compassion for *your own mind* as you train it. As I've said, if you start to train a puppy and immediately expect it to do tricks, do a "down-stay" for an hour, or some other such demand, you're going to have a neurotic puppy that absolutely hates training sessions. It will be a fighting match all the way. Given the power of the human unconscious mind, I guarantee that if you take such a demanding and merciless approach to practice, you'll make no progress and you'll eventually give up practice altogether.

> "Meditation is really just learning to enjoy your experience, so you don't have to tense up. Don't make meditation a project like everything else."
>
> *Elizabeth Mattis-Namgyel*

Remember, it's taken you lifetimes to get to this opportunity. Moving forward five minutes at a time now is still more progress than you've made in, literally, ages.

The good news is that if you don't push yourself unrealistically, practice sessions can feel good. Really good.

Something the Tibetans call the Four Thoughts also puts us into the proper frame of mind. It actually *uses* our natural tendency to think about things. It brings even that onto the path, and we emerge from these four contemplations having a much clearer, broader, and deeper understanding of our place in the great scheme of things. This helps not only with practice but with life. I want to remind you of the woman whose sister had suddenly died. She said that it was mostly having contemplated the Four Thoughts that had served her so well in her grief. Without having expanded her worldview and brought it into focus, she would have handled her sister's death badly. None of us knows when something tragic like that will happen to us. We can only know that eventually something will happen. Such is life.

Even when nothing terrible is happening, to have consciously and thoroughly worked out your worldview is a satisfying thing. We haven't had much opportunity or guidance in the past, so here's an opportunity to really dive into it.

In Closing—
Some Words of Advice

Now that you've taken in a feast of new information, it's time to digest. Please take your time with the vast wealth of knowledge and skillful means that you've just perused. Again, study, contemplate, revisit, and practice it all—doing the Round Robin Meditation, or doing full sessions on whatever you're working on, if that works better for you. Take to heart whichever concepts ring true (and keep an open mind and heart for those that still seem to be a stretch).

After you've drunk deeply of these ideas and practices for a few months, you'll have just *begun* to taste the benefits. Trust me on this one. Better yet, *don't* trust me. Keep on with these practices and see for yourself!

It doesn't matter how smart or how spiritual you are—charging ahead will be of little benefit. In fact, the more seriously you want to pursue this, the more you'll get out of these thoughts and methods by going bit by bit, sinking deeply into each part.

During the course of your day, try out some understanding you've achieved in meditation. Or, going the other way, as you witness or experience events, or interact with others, see if any of your recent understandings shed light on these moments. The illumination could come from your Tonglen practice, from the Four Thoughts, from Shamata.

There are many, many fine nuggets of understanding to be found, one by one, as you read, contemplate, and practice. With these nuggets you can build a worldview that's fully considered, tested, and made your own. Why rush?

If you build a hasty foundation, your house won't be straight or stand very long.

From another point of view, I hope you're enjoying the *doing* of these contemplations and practices, enjoying the adventure of inquiry. I hope you're finding meaning in the ideas you've encountered, and I sincerely hope you study further from other books and especially real, live teachers. This book was never intended to give you all of even the foundational understandings.

A Word or Two about Drugs

I'm speaking of the "recreational" kind. Often, while you're on whatever it is, you think you're seeing the world more clearly. Sometimes you may indeed get a glimpse of something—sort of like walking in the middle of the forest and then climbing a tree. Maybe we can see much farther, but, even then, we still have to climb down and keep walking if we're ever going to get "home."

In most cases, though, if we think we're brilliant when we write that poem while high, we read it in the morning and it's incomprehensible or embarrassing—or both. Or while we were drunk, other people— who weren't—saw us not as clever and charming but as slobbery and obnoxious.

One fellow, who had been meditating for years and was very fond of his dope, had this to say: "Meditating, then getting high, is like washing your white pants, putting them on, and then sitting in the mud." Another indulger of similar habits confessed that getting drunk or high was like putting a paper bag over his head. Perhaps not an effective enlightenment technique.

If you honestly want to give the things in this book a real try, you won't even know what they can do for you, much less actually derive a whole lot of benefit, if you cause more mental obscuration with drugs. Our windshields are already smeared with Samsaric gunk—we don't need to slather on another layer of drug sludge. It's simply the opposite direction from the one you're trying to pursue.

But let's face it: We all, in one form or another, take refuge in some form of addiction, and it's very hard to stop. This is a kind of catch-22 again. As with the greater catch-22 I talked about, you can work slowly and consistently with your mind on this. As in my case with cigarettes, I'm hoping that, as you do practice, you get *enough* benefit that you can begin to take refuge in the experiences you're having in practice instead of your addiction of choice. Probably the thing I felt most immediately happy about, once I no longer smoked, was that I was no longer a slave to it. I was free.

In addressing your addictions, you can, of course, complement your practice with other resources. Support groups such as Alcoholics Anonymous, and other programs with similar approaches, have helped many free themselves from addiction. Their tenets can dovetail quite nicely with the worldview and methods presented here.

As I've mentioned, my worst addiction when I started Buddhist practice was smoking. I couldn't stop, even though I was terrified of cancer. Nicotine is a kind of speed, and it's more addictive than heroin. If you decide to quit smoking, you might find that a nicotine patch helps you during the first week or so.

And for other addictions or self-destructive patterns, you can seek out alternatives, methods, and support to help you get unstuck and moving forward.

If you already have something larger you can go to for refuge—something beyond the vicissitudes of everyday, problematic life and death—then you could pray fervently to them. If you don't already have something, then you could try using the image I've included in the packet at the back of the book. The great, wise, loving emptiness is hard for us to relate to directly, so an image can really help. This one is of the primordial Buddha (Sanskrit for "awakened one") in male and female form—our original source—our original mother and father.

I hope all this helps you. After all, the whole point is to *clear away* obscurations, and given what you know now, wouldn't you be really sad to see all or part of your efforts go to waste?

More Support—Why Not?

While you're spending your time plumbing the depths of these under-standings and practices, I encourage you to read other books and go to teaching and practice retreats. (As the band U2 notes in one of its songs: "You don't have to go it alone.")

True, practicing alone has its particular rewards, but you can get other benefits from practicing and discussing in a group. Why not have both? If there's a Vajrayana group in your area that you feel an affinity for, try one of their meetings. If not, you might put a posting on the internet and start your own study group, using this book and others I've mentioned.

If you need help finding others to practice and study with, you can contact the Namchak Foundation (Namchak.org), and we can help you locate students near you. Over the years I've found that by sit-ting with others and studying and practicing together, you're much more likely to make much more progress. In fact, without the support of fellow travelers, I found that almost every single student stopped altogether.

In my own experience, of course, Tulku Sangak Rinpoche is an expert at all of these practices, he's the world lineage holder, and his motivation is impeccable. His teaching is both laser-sharp and utterly kindhearted, his sense of humor and play unfailing. I know for sure that he exemplifies the teachings in his life story and behavior. These days Rinpoche doesn't teach the foundational practices very often, but he has asked me to. If you'd like to come to one of my retreats, please do visit the Namchak website to learn more.*

---

*   Missoula, MT, practitioners can visit the Ewam.org website.

In recent years, Rinpoche has asked his brother Khen Rinpoche—a scholar and highly accomplished practitioner—to teach the foundational practices, along with others. The brothers are very much alike, not only in their practical and focused presentation, but in their kindness and humor. You can learn more about Khen Rinpoche on the Namchak website.

I've appreciated sticking mainly with one teacher who can teach me everything, and one particular lineage, so that I don't waste too much time with distraction along the path. The downside for you is that as a result I don't have much experience of other Sanghas and teachers. Though I've heard of several Sanghas and teachers in America, I hesitate to recommend any one of them I haven't experienced myself and can't confidently give my recommendation for.

I will recommend a few resources that I do know about, but my knowledge is limited.

That said, the books that I recommend can really help you along the way—and keep your monkey mind entertained! Of course they'll enrich your practice and your view of reality. Beyond that you'll encounter the wisdom of great masters, both past and present. Why not let them help you directly with your practice?

The other thing I want to stress, as you do these practices, is the importance of studying with actual, qualified masters. Even if you don't have one in a neighborhood near you, you can still make leaps and bounds of progress in your practice with their help by reading a book they've written or traveling to one of their retreats.

And only qualified masters can teach you the next level of practices, the Ngöndro. Once you've decided to really give these a try, then you need to give yourself a chance to feel their effects.

Do yourself a favor, then, and—for now—resist the temptation to move on to teachings on yet other practices. If you try to move ahead too quickly, you'll risk letting these foundational practices go to waste without having really given them a chance to work—or perhaps without even fully absorbing them, like studying quadratic equations before being reliably able to multiply and divide.

The result will almost certainly be distraction from forward motion on your journey—a waste of your precious time. Probably the most important loss would be that you would have started building the walls of the house before finishing the foundation.

So be here now, and stay here for a while.

Some of my fellow Sangha members wondered how I'd made such steady progress on the path. There were three reasons, none mysterious or impressive:

1. I stayed with one practice and just focused on that until Rinpoche gave me the next one.
2. I didn't go to any teachings or empowerments—even Rinpoche's—that weren't "on topic" for what I was actually studying or practicing at the time.
3. I spent a whole lot of time doing practice and trying my best.

(HINT: I made the most progress on retreats. Just as total immersion is really the best way to learn a new language, total immersion in the practices works best too, for the same reasons.)

Given how precious *all* of the teachings and empowerments are, you might be wondering why I chose such a focused, seemingly narrow and restricted approach, why I decided to follow ONE path up the mountain, despite the fact that many of them would lead me there.

Well, I was daunted by the hours it would take to apply even the foundational practices to the challenge of changing the habits of my mind. When we hear about the various practices, texts, and empowerments, we can feel like a kid in a candy store (or a vegan at an organic farmers' market): so many delightful options, and we want to sample them all. But I thought that my most direct route to the most potent practices and eventual enlightenment was to focus on one particular set of practices, laid out by my Root Lama, and to pursue them without any sidetracks. I believe that even Dharma can be a distraction if it's not on our own particular step-by-step path.

Empowerments

Before I give you the names of some teachers, I want to offer another piece of advice. As you explore Vajrayana, you'll probably encounter a concept called *wang** in Tibetan, or "empowerment" in English. Again, in most cases I'd think twice before giving in to the temptation to dash off to one of these empowerments. I'll explain wangs more fully in a future book, but for now I'll just say that they can sometimes be another distraction at best. Since at a wang you're making a deep connection between your mind and the lama's, you want to be very sure this is what you want—and that lama is who you want to connect with.

Since you're also deeply connecting with a deity at a wang, you want to make sure you really plan to uphold the vows you take at that time—and, at wangs, there always are vows. The breaking of vows is not exactly good karma.

One common vow is to do the practice the wang was intended for, every day for the rest of your life. I knew one practitioner who had gone to many wangs. She would sit with a huge pile of practice texts from the various empowerments, spending so many hours keeping her accumulated vows every day that she never had a chance to finish her Ngöndro, much less the practices beyond that, even after many years.

With that caution in mind, there are some very basic empowerments that just bring the blessings of enlightened beings to you,

---

* *Abisheka* in Sanskrit, sometimes called "transmission" in English. It is a ceremony empowering someone to pursue a particular path of practice, and to enter the mandala—the inner world, so to speak—of a particular deity.

without heavy commitments or prerequisites. The category to look in, at this point, would be the ones from the outer tantras. Some—though not all—of the Green Tara, Chenrezi (Avalokitesvara), Medicine Buddha, Amitabha, and Amitayus empowerments would fall into this category. Be sure to ask about vows and prerequisites before deciding to go. Do your best to make sure the lama is one you want to have that deep, mind-to-mind connection with. If you're satisfied that there are no drawbacks to going—no excessive commitments that you can't realistically keep, no prerequisites you haven't met, no doubts about the lama leading the empowerment—then you might as well take in the benefits.

The *reasons* to go to a wang are many and compelling. First of all, since the qualified vajra master giving the wang has joined his or her mind with the lamas of the lineage before, tracing all the way back to the primordial Buddha, the blessings are huge. Through extremely refined and skillful means, the enlightened minds of these beings are transferred to you. It's as though a seed for enlightenment is planted within your mindstream, as are the particular archetypal qualities of the deities involved, who are also enlightened beings.

Often you will need the wang to open up your mindstream to a whole cycle of teachings, if you intend to do any study or practice within that cycle. For all of these reasons I hope that you do go to the occasional empowerment. While I was doing the Ngöndro, I went to outer tantra wangs for very few deities, mostly the ones included in the Ngöndro practices. Since in this case there were no vows to do some added practice, I just received the blessings of the lama, the lineages, and the deities. I need all the support I can get, in improving my mind, so I was delighted to see how much these wangs boosted my efforts.

Refuge Ceremony

If you decide that you want to pursue this path further, then one thing that *will* help you, at this point and in the future, is the Refuge Ceremony. For that you'll need a qualified lama. I've been using the term *qualified lama* a lot but haven't defined it yet. I will go into that in the "Guru Yoga" section later in this series, so when you have that, you can sneak a peek there before deciding on a Refuge Ceremony. You can also read about the attributes of a qualified lama in the first part of *The Words of My Perfect Teacher* by Patrul Rinpoche.

Through such a lama you can connect your mind with the lineage of Buddhist masters all the way back to the Buddha. You get the support of that connection for the rest of your life and plant the seeds of enlightenment for the future. All of this happens in the Refuge Ceremony. Once you're ready, you might want to avail yourself of it. If so, it wouldn't hurt to read the corresponding chapter in *The Words of My Perfect Teacher*, and I'll have a chapter on refuge in Book 3.

More about the Three Jewels

You might be wondering exactly *what*, in the Refuge Ceremony, you'll be taking refuge *in*. Well, it won't be the things of Samsara—that's what you're taking refuge *from*. We've tried that for a few billion aeons and it hasn't really worked out. We might do well to pick something beyond the bounds of Samsara, something most likely to succeed.

If you're going on a long, confusing, sometimes difficult journey, you'll want a few essentials. First would be a guide—not just any guide, but someone who has successfully traveled to your destination. A distant second choice might be someone who hasn't gotten all the way there themselves but is confident that they know how to get there. In this case, the Buddha is obviously the first choice: he has fully succeeded in reaching the goal of liberation. For this reason he's the first of the Three Jewels.

Second, you'll want some advice and information on how to reach your destination: a map, directions about the tricky parts, and advice on how to successfully move along down the road. And, of course, you're going to need a vehicle too. All this corresponds to the second Jewel, the Dharma. The Buddha not only traversed the path to enlightenment, he showed us the path, in several styles—Theravada, Mahayana, and Vajrayana (remember, *yana* means "vehicle"). And there are subgroups within those groups (a vehicle lot full of an array of road-tested choices, complete with Samsaric windshield wipers).

And you'll want traveling companions. Traveling alone is more arduous, not much fun, and sometimes outright dangerous. So the third Jewel is the Sangha. If you pick friends who are going in a different direction than you're headed, with a different goal, how is that going to help you on the way to *your* goal? This is a painful truth sometimes, but I couldn't not mention it to you. Please take a good, honest look at who you're marinating your mind with these days.

Thoughts and points of view are infectious.

Once you've found your traveling companions, you'll have resources you can share, you'll encourage each other when one of you gets discouraged, and you'll keep each other enthused about the journey and the goal. If one of you stumbles or gets hurt, the others will be there

to help. Then there's the sheer joy of sharing the wonders of the journey. When you experience something in practice—joyful or painful—a fellow Sangha member will understand in a particular way. They might even have something especially helpful for you because they share much of your worldview and a common "language" for talking about such things.

A variety of factors contribute to the powerful human instinct for groupthink. We like to see ourselves as above that, but biology and instinct create a very powerful tide pulling us into, and holding us within, the group. Humans have been herd animals for millions of years. For almost every bit of that time, being outside the tribe meant certain death. Jung invented many new terms as he mapped out the human psyche for us Westerners. One term, *centroversion*, is the human tendency to think like those around us.

While identifying with the group can be motivating and reassuring, once a practitioner is quite accomplished, it's recommended that they get beyond the gravitational pull of other people. At a certain point, when we're really starting to move beyond an ordinary perception of the world, sometimes even fellow Sangha members can hold us back. Then solitary retreat in a wild place is recommended.

So for you, if you're hanging out in bars a lot, do you think that would have the same effect as going to Sangha meetings and practicing together, talking about life in ways you all understand, working together on some projects, and studying Dharma books together?

I'm not suggesting you get up from reading this book and promptly divorce your spouse and drop your friends. But if you'd like some support on your journey, I recommend that you find a group in your area. If there is no group, you could always start one. Remember that our website can help you find either an existing group, or other people interested in starting one. We also have audio, visual, and written materials to make it easier to start and conduct a group.

Speaking of Sangha, I thought I should mention my own. The entire Sangha is international, with monasteries and lay communities in Asia as well as the US. The spiritual leader of all of our communities is Tulku Sangak Rinpoche because he is the world lineage holder of the Namchak Lineage.

Some of our centers, not surprisingly, have *Namchak* in their names, while others have the word *Ewam*. Both names have been used historically to describe our lineage, and they're all part of this larger Sangha, under Rinpoche's spiritual leadership.

You can also visit Namchak.org for a brief history of our lineage, a "family tree" of the lineage holders tracing back to Guru Rinpoche, and more up-to-date information on the centers and the various activities. We also have an online store, where you can browse for practice items, beautiful scroll paintings called *tangkas*, CDs, DVDs, and books. See you there!

What Will Refuge in the Three Jewels Do for Me?

You can get some idea of the benefits of taking refuge in the Three Jewels from the explanations above. Beyond that, though, there is the subtle but huge support of *all* those who have ever taken refuge in those same Three Jewels. That's a lot of people. It includes all those who achieved Buddhahood, and all of the bodhisattvas. The numbers are impossible to count.

According to Rupert Sheldrake's theory of morphic resonance, that non-local wisdom, compassion, and support are there for you wherever you are. The ceremony plugs you into that greater Sangha—and that's a really big Sangha!

Once you've vowed to take refuge in those Three Jewels, you renew that vow every day. This serves to strengthen that plugging-in to the legions of wise ones and fellow travelers. It's not easy, by any means, to crowbar ourselves out of our entrenched habits. It's not even easy to do daily meditation. Heck, we have trouble even quieting our minds for a whole breath! I don't know about you, but I want all the help I can get. Remember . . .

Thoughts and points of view are infectious.

Might as well have that work *for* us.

And when the things of Samsara that we find ourselves secretly leaning on let us down—and sooner or later they always do—in the end, this is something we can turn to, something we can count on.

Sure, it's not easy to see, taste, or feel the Three Jewels . . . in the beginning. That's why they're represented in various ways—to help us find a way to perceive them. For example, the picture of the Happy Couple, as I call them, on the Vajradhara & Mandharava visualization card which I gave you, represents the Three Jewels. They're enlightened beings, so their minds are the Jewel of the Buddha, their speech is the Dharma, and their bodies are the Sangha.

The same is true of your Root Lama: their body is the Sangha, their speech is the Dharma, and their mind, on an ultimate level, is Buddha Mind. Because of who they are and all the work they've done, less gets in the way of your seeing that. Of course, how well you can see the Three Jewels manifested in them still largely depends on the level of your own obscurations and your own capacity for what's called *pure vision.*

You want to practice that with your fellow Sangha members too. That won't always be easy. That's why they call it *practice.* But it's a very worthy cause. Just think: if you all practiced pure vision with each other, how lovely that would feel for all of you. And your work would go well too. This is absolutely a part of the path. As a matter of fact, purifying our vision is a major feature of Vajrayana.

How Will I Know if I'm Ready to Take Refuge?

I have no idea.

Sorry. I can only tell you when I felt *I* was ready. When I had looked at other paths and found they weren't for me, and this one made sense to me, I decided to road test it. And I felt the only way to do that was to actually plunge in and experience it fully. At that point I took refuge and dived into the practices, met with others, took occasional teachings, and studied. All of these elements supported and guided me, and I found that this path was really helping me. I don't know how else I would have known for sure.

More Follow-Through: Some Qualified Teachers

Back to the teaching retreats: they *will* help you. Obviously you want ones that focus on the practices you've been reading about, as well as those that give you more general background on Buddhism. If you like the approach of Vajrayana (Tibetan Buddhism), you'll want to focus on ones that fall within that. The Dharma is so vast that you could easily get confused if you sample different approaches without exploring any one of them fully or deeply. Since the Buddha intended for each yana to fit a particular type of person, the concepts of one can sometimes seem to contradict the other. You do want to make sure you've found the yana that works for you, but once you've done so, stick with it. Interestingly, His Holiness the Dalai Lama advises this approach even more broadly to followers of non-Buddhist spiritual traditions: if it (whatever religion or philosophy *it* may be) is working for you, you're probably best off continuing to follow its precepts.

Our Namchak Foundation, as well as Ewam, offers teaching retreats on the basic practices offered in this book, as well as others. Tulku Sangak Rinpoche himself taught them for many years, but now he focuses more on the advanced practices. We need him to! His brother Khen Rinpoche teaches more advanced practices and some that beginners can do as well.

Rinpoche has asked me to teach the foundational ones included in this book as well as such topics as the Seven Point Mind Training, which is also a foundational practice that takes the practices I've introduced in this book and helps us apply them to our everyday lives. I've mentioned that I teach the Ngöndro, or Preliminary Practices, as well. I would recommend doing the practices in this book for at least six months to a year before moving on to the Ngöndro. Of course you're welcome to come to any of our beginning-level retreats that are appropriate. (If you're not sure whether a retreat would be a good fit for you, please contact us—or whoever might be holding the retreat, if it's elsewhere—and ask.)

I'd be happy to see you there! We do a lot of learning, learn a lot of doing, and have a lot of fun doing it.

If you can't or don't want to go to one of those offered through the Namchak Foundation or Ewam, you could go to one offered by Anam Thubten Rinpoche. He is also both an erudite scholar and an accomplished practitioner. An added benefit is that he speaks excellent English.

Another qualified master is Mingyur Rinpoche, and he teaches this level, as do some of his advanced students. He also speaks English, and of course his American students who teach do too!

There are probably other qualified teachers of beginning Vajrayana out there, but as I said, I don't get out much. I don't feel I can recommend a teacher or Sangha without having some personal experience with them and their teachings—so if I don't mention here someone who appeals to you, I'm not *not* recommending them; I just don't know enough to have an informed opinion (which is really the best kind to have).

I also lead monthly meditation coaching calls. Please check the Namchak website for details.

The Next Step—When You're Really Ready

I'm hoping this book helps you be a happier person. That would make *me* happy.

If you read this book, try the methods for a while, and find you're really interested in pursuing this path further, you'll need some support on your way.

First and most essentially, as I've said, you'll need a qualified teacher. Second, you'll want to take the Refuge Vows.

Third, once you've done these practices for at least six months to a year, and if you want to pursue Vajrayana, the traditional next step is the Ngöndro, or Preliminary Practices. The word *preliminary* doesn't refer to their being simple or remedial. They're a collection of practices that are a microcosm of the entire Vajrayana path. They're considered so essential that they're done either at the beginning of, or before, any other practices, and before starting one's day. *That's* what's meant by *preliminary*.

The Ngöndro practice texts are specifically designed to be supports and reminders for the *lama's teachings*. In many cases, even though the teacher may not have been ordained a lama, they will still be highly qualified. You simply have to look at their qualifications, both inner and outer, and judge if they're right for you. The Ngöndro text in my next book is meant almost as a reminder or reference—to bring the lama's full teachings to mind when you're doing your daily practice. It's not meant to replace the lama's live teachings—and neither is this book, for that matter (although I am a live lama!).

Without that personal, in-person interaction with a teacher, you're missing crucial pieces and the Ngöndro simply won't work for you in the way it's intended. The Ngöndro is strong medicine, and you don't want to take it without seeing the doctor and getting their instructions.

The practices I give in this book can be done without a qualified teacher's instruction without much risk of harm. But if you try them and like them, why not get more support, help, and clarity from a qualified teacher for these too? This book, along with *Why Bother?*, is not the only reading you'll need, either. In Appendix C: Recommended Reading, I list and talk a bit about some excellent books that can further your understanding.

And for those of you who find this is your cup of tea and would like to learn and practice further, the additional books in this series, as they become available, will present the next sets of practices. The medicine gets progressively stronger as we go along. Rinpoche has taught me all of the levels of this path, as he has for many others. Not only has he authorized me to teach all of the foundational practices, he fully *expects* me to teach them. That works for me—there's nothing I like better!

For now you have quite a few new understandings, methods, and resources—congratulations! It's a little like you've been given recipes, and you even have the ingredients. Now if you cook them up and actually *eat* them . . . then give yourself some time to *chew and digest* . . . wouldn't that be lovely? Isn't that the best part of a recipe?

In the large view you've now considered, you might ask yourself the question I've asked myself so many times, over the years:

"Do I have something *better* to do?"

Appendix A: How to Find or Start a Learning Circle (Practice Group)

Here are a few ideas to help you find fellow adventurers, and to help you all begin and continue the exploration together. Of course, you can all use this book as part of that exploration. You can read a bit during the week, then gather to discuss that bit, seeing what gem of understanding you create when you share all your varied facets of understanding. Or you might want just to read a few pages together, to discuss. You can find a companion workbook on namchakpublishing.com, full of reflection questions and discussion prompts.

To keep things focused, I recommend following the simple agenda I've outlined below. You could trade off being the person to lead you all through it. When I was doing three-month-long retreats, that's what our weekly group did. At the beginning of the three months, each member signed up for a particular time. It worked quite well, and everyone became very close.

During the meetings you can talk together about each of your life's challenges and how these understandings and methods are, or aren't, working for you. You offer each other your simple, caring support.

Then you meditate together, a beautiful experience like none other—sharing the silence. I've included a simple guide below that leaves lots of room for your own group's creativity and personality.

But how do you find such a group if you don't happen to have one handy? This modern world, where we don't even know most of our neighbors' names, doesn't make it easy. But there's a very modern solution: the Internet. If you write to Info@Namchak.org, we can help you to find an existing group, or at least others in your area or online. We can send you a Toolkit to help you get started, and/or you can join a small group of fellow newcomers online, who are exploring the idea.

As I've said in various ways in this book, I believe that our modern society got confused along the way. We made the mistake of substituting money and prestige for meaning. This served to isolate us. We became isolated from the human beings around us, the other beings around us, and the whole environment. Has this served to bring us happiness? We thought it would, but we have come to the logical end of this pursuit. It hasn't brought us our desired goal of happiness, but is destroying the planet, creatures, other people, and left us with little meaning to our lives. Many have found that these Learning Circles have brought deep meaning and connection to their lives. I wish that for you.

We also believe strongly in Engaged Bodhicitta. "Bodhicitta" means "awakening heart/mind." Bodhicitta is being awake to our not being separate. The two kinds of Bodhicitta are Aspirational and Engaged. With Aspirational, we utilize our practices to expand our inner capacity for connection. Once you've developed those resources a bit, you're ready to add the Engaged Bodhicitta. At this point, you're naturally inspired to get up and act from that love and compassion. We recommend devoting some meetings to everyone seeing what they want to offer to a world in need, and support each other in those efforts. Here's a very simple template to use with a Learning Circle, with this or another book as a basis of study.

Learning Circle Meeting

- A few minutes of silence.
- Give rise to altruistic motivation.
- Share community agreements.
- Each person checks in:
  - *How are you doing with the Practice of Doing Daily Practice?*
  - *Do you see any connections between your practice on the cushion and your life off the cushion?*

- Read a few pages from a selected text or watch a video from the eCourse.
- Discussion. *How does this relate to your life?*
  - *If your group is more than 6 people, you may want to break into groups of 2 or 4 to allow for equal sharing of voices.*

- Group mediation for 20 minutes. Shamata, Tonglen, or Round Robin.
- A few minutes of chanting, if you like.

Dedication and Aspiration

By the power of this compassionate practice
May suffering be transformed into peace.
May the hearts of all beings be open,
And their wisdom radiate from within.

Additional guidance and material for Learning Circles at Namchak.org

Appendix B: Glossary

Absolute Truth (Tibetan: *dön-dam-denba*): The abiding truth, not subject to a particular deluded being's point of view. The reality perceived by enlightened beings. *See also* Two Truths.

Archetype: Jungian term describing a sort of lens that acts as a template, shaping generalized consciousness into a more particular principle of reality with particular characteristics—for example, the Great Mother archetype or the Wise Man archetype—which one can find in images and stories throughout human societies.

Bardo (Tibetan; literally "between two"): Generally used to refer to the dreamlike state between lifetimes. Technically we experience other bardos, such as the time in between birth and death.

Bodhicitta [bo-di-CHIT-ta] (Sanskrit; "Mind of Enlightenment/Awakening"): "On the relative level, it is the wish to attain Buddhahood for the sake of all beings, as well as the practice of the path of love, compassion, the six transcendent perfections, etc., necessary for achieving that goal. On the absolute level, it is the direct insight into the ultimate nature." (From *The Words of My Perfect Teacher* by Patrul Rinpoche, trans., Padmakhara Translation Group.) It is the motivation to help others. It naturally flows from our own Buddha Nature, which *feels* how we're not separate from others.

Bodhisattva [bo-di-SAT-va] (Sanskrit): One who is primarily motivated by bodhicitta. There are many levels of bodhisattva, depending on the spiritual achievement of such a being.

Buddha (Sanskrit; "Awakened One"): A being who has reached full enlightenment by cleansing all adventitious *lo-bur* ("baggage"), such as karma and bad habits of the mind, and has fully brought forth—matured—their Buddha Nature. It is predicted that there will be over a thousand who will reach this state in this *kalpa*, or aeon. Note: The buddha who created the religion and methods of Buddhism and taught the sutras and tantras was the Buddha Shakyamuni.

Buddha Nature (Tibetan: *deshek nyingpo*): Our essential nature, which is not separate from the Dharmakaya and is the seed of our own complete enlightenment.

Dharma (Sanskrit): A general term for the teachings and path of the Buddha Shakyamuni.

Dharmakaya (Sanskrit; literally "Truth Body"): The vast, pregnant emptiness out of which everything arises. It is not a dead vacuum, but pure, essential awareness. It is beyond defining but has many qualities. It is vast without limit; ultimate compassion, ultimate unity, pure potential, all-knowing, the ultimate root of all. At this level there is no form; there is unity. It is no different from complete Buddhahood.

Five Dhyani Buddha Families: For each of these five categories, or families, there is a particular buddha, color, direction, and many other characteristics. These are the Sanskrit Buddha Family names (male, female).

1. Buddha: Vairochana, Dhatishvari
2. Lotus: Amitabha, Pandaravasini
3. Vajra: Akshobhya, Buddhalochana
4. Jewel: Ratnasambhava, Mamaki
5. Karma: Amogasiddhi, Samayatara

These are also listed in the same order as the Five Poisons (see below). The Five Buddha Families weave together, along with all their qualities and characteristics, to create the complex appearances of manifested reality.

Five Poisons: The five neurotic emotions that usually motivate the thoughts, speech, and actions of sentient beings. The Buddha spoke of 84,000 of them, but they are generally grouped into these categories:

1. Ignorance, stupor, laziness, dullness, narrow-mindedness, etc.
2. Clinging, desire, longing, addiction, etc.
3. Aversion, aggression, fear, hatred, worry, etc.
4. Pride, ego inflation (a subcategory of no. 3)
5. Jealousy, competitiveness (also a subcategory of no. 3)

When we speak of the *Three Poisons*, we're to understand that no. 4 and no. 5 are subsumed under no. 3.

Five Primordial Yeshes: The first division into multiplicity, emanating from the unified nature of the Dharmakaya. Yeshe divides into its five basic aspects, like facets of one jewel. This is on the Sambhogakaya level. Each of the Five Poisons, without its adventitious, deluded element—in other words, in its pure essence—is one of the Five Primordial Yeshes. Below they are listed in the order in which the Five Poisons were listed:

1. Yeshe of Basic Space
2. Discerning Yeshe
3. Mirrorlike Yeshe
4. Equalizing Yeshe
5. All-Accomplishing Yeshe

Four Thoughts: The longer term is "Four Thoughts That Turn the Mind (from Samsara)." This is a group of four contemplations that, from four different entry points, guide us in a thorough exploration of our larger situation within Samsara.

Karma (Sanskrit; "action"): In this context it refers not only to actions but to their natural consequential effects. Think "Ye shall reap what ye sow."

Lama (Tibetan): A title equivalent to *rabbi* or *minister*. In Vajrayana the lama is often more of a spiritual mentor than their Christian counterpart or than in Theravada Buddhism.

Mahayana (Sanskrit; "Great Vehicle"): That branch of Buddhism which has the Two Purposes as motivating factors: enlightenment for self *and* for others.

In every school of Mahayana Buddhism, one takes a vow to help *all* beings toward enlightenment.

Mala: A garland of beads used by Buddhists, and those of other spiritual traditions, to track repetitions during prayer or meditation.

Marigpa (Tibetan): Lack of awareness. Usually translated as "ignorance."

Merit: Positive effects of actions, in particular. Like an entry appearing in the credit column of the karmic "ledger."

Mindstream: That bit of awareness that inhabits the body but isn't actually *of* the body, and that experiences lifetime after lifetime.

Ngöndro [NGÖN-dro] (Tibetan; "Preliminary Practices"): These are practiced after Shiney and before more advanced practices. Actually, Ngöndro is incorporated into the beginning of advanced practices too—hence the name.

Nirmanakaya (Sanskrit; "Emanation Body"): The manifestation level/aspect of shining forth from the Dharmakaya/Buddhahood. Another, further order of complexity of form, as compared with the Sambhogakaya. Perceptible to sentient beings in a warped and confused way, depending on their own karmically and habitually distorted "lens."

Original Purity (Tibetan: *kadak*): An intrinsic quality of the Dharmakaya, and all that issues from it. This, of course, includes human beings.

Relative Truth (Tibetan: *kün dzop denba*): The reality perceived by sentient beings, in their deluded state. *See also* Two Truths.

Rinpoche [RIN-po-chey]: An honorific term used for high lamas—higher than the Christian term *reverend*, but lower than *His Holiness*. Most lamas are not referred to by this title, only the most accomplished.

Root Lama: Root guru. An individual spiritual guide and mentor. This is arguably the most intimate and karmically significant of human relationships.

Sambhogakaya (Sanskrit; literally "Body of Complete Enjoyment"): The first level/aspect of spontaneous shining forth into form, from the Dharmakaya. Similar to the archetypal level of being that Jungians speak of. Rarely directly perceptible to human beings.

Samsara (Sanskrit): The cycle of existence—of birth, death, and rebirth—in which all sentient beings find ourselves. We are propelled from one situation to the next by our own deluded thoughts, negative emotions, karma, and habits of mind, from which we perform actions that, in turn, create further karmic consequences. We then react to these, mentally, emotionally, and physically. These in turn create ceaseless experiences in existence, like a self-perpetuating dream, until we finally wake up (and, as His Holiness the Dalai Lama says, "Better it be sooner").

Sangha (Sanskrit): The spiritual community.

Shamata (Sanskrit; "Tranquil Abiding Meditation"; Tibetan: *Shiney*): A meditation that is practiced, in similar forms, in all branches of Buddhism. It is taught to new practitioners in Vajrayana. Its endeavor is to calm the flow of thoughts while heightening mindfulness. Eventually, through this training, one can focus attention on one thing and have it stay there, in a clear, unperturbed, joyfully peaceful state.

Sublime Insight (Sanskrit: *Pali, Vipassana, Vipashyana*): This is usually practiced in conjunction with Tranquil Abiding, Shamata. Both of these practices are found in all branches of Buddhism. In Vajrayana they're seen as foundational and necessary, but as a means to further practices. In a commonly used analogy, Shamata and Vipassana are like the foundation of a house, which must be well established before the walls and the roof are added.

Sutra [SOO-tra]: The original teachings of the Buddha.

Tantra [TAHN-tra]: Further teachings of the Buddha, which are not studied or practiced by the Theravadins but are the mainstay of Vajrayana— Tibetan Buddhism.

Theravada [teh-ra-VA-da] (Sanskrit; "Root, or Foundational Vehicle, School of the Elders"): The foundational-level branch of Buddhism, common to all branches. Of the three main branches of teachings of the Buddha Shakyamuni, it was the first to be taught. It is based on the sutras, and does not include the tantras; the motivation for enlightenment is focused on one's own liberation from Samsara.

Three Jewels: The Buddha, the Dharma, and the Sangha—in which all Buddhists have vowed to take refuge until reaching complete enlightenment. The thought is that the combination of all three will greatly help us along the way: the Buddha because he has achieved enlightenment himself, so has proven to know the way; the Dharma because it is the instructions, or "map," that he provided us; and the Sangha, or spiritual community, as companions along the way.

Three Kayas: *See* Dharmakaya, Sambhogakaya, Nirmanakaya.

Three Poisons, a.k.a. *afflictive emotions* (Tibetan: *nyön-mong*): The Buddha (Shakyamuni) grouped the thousands of emotions like fear, worry, longing, etc., into three basic categories:

1. Ignorance, delusion, laziness, narrow-mindedness, and similar emotions
2. Desire, clinging, longing, and such
3. Aversion, aggression, hatred, dislike, fear, and such

Sometimes they are spoken of as the Five Poisons (see entry above), with the fourth and fifth categories under the third category, anger/aversion. The fourth is pride, inflation, and such, and the fifth is jealousy, competitiveness, and such. They are often subsumed under the third category because they are considered to be forms or subsets of anger/aversion.

Tonglen (Tibetan; "Sending and Receiving"): A compassion practice in which one breathes in the suffering of others and breathes out happiness toward them.

Tulku [TOOL-koo] (Tibetan; "Emanation Body"; Sanskrit: *Nirmanakaya*): An individual who has mastered their mind enough that they can control their landing in their next incarnation. The tulku system has been used in Tibet for heads of monasteries and sub-lineages to allow them to shoulder their responsibilities for many lifetimes. This is why His Holiness the Dalai Lama XIV is referred to as the fourteenth: he has been recognized and has held the Office of the Dalai Lama thirteen previous times.

Two Truths (Tibetan: *denba nyi*): The two aspects of reality, like two sides of one coin. These two aspects are called Relative Truth (*kün dzop denba*) and Absolute Truth, or Ultimate Truth (*dön-dam denba*).

Vajrayana: A branch of Mahayana, which uses many skillful means from the tantras to pursue enlightenment more efficiently. It is the branch of Buddhism generally practiced by Tibetans.

Vipassana (Tibetan: *Lhaktong*; "Sublime Insight"): Usually practiced along with Shamata/Shiney. The practice of seeing the true nature of either the object of our attention or us ourselves.

Wang, Lung: These are two kinds of transmissions that a lama gives to students, to connect and open their minds in a profound way to a particular cycle of teachings and/or practices.

Yeshe: Also called timeless awareness or (primordial) wisdom. The wisdom inherent in the Dharmakaya, which shines forth into all of its created emanations.

Yidam: Deity practice. One meditates on a particular realized being who personifies a particular aspect of wisdom—an archetypal image. It is widely practiced in Vajrayana.

Appendix C: Recommended Reading

FOR PRACTICE & GENERAL READING

Tulku Sangak Rinpoche. *Distilled Nectar from the Lips of the Lama, the Lord Protector Manjushri: The Way to Develop Calm Abiding and Profound Insight.* Missoula, MT: Namchak Publishing, 2021. You can purchase through Namchak Publishing (NamchakPublishing.com).

Matthieu Ricard. *Happiness.* English language edition. New York: Little, Brown and Company, 2006. This book does a beautiful job of answering the question, "Tibetan Buddhism—why bother?" Ricard was at Dilgo Khyentse Rinpoche's side since before Tulku Sangak Rinpoche arrived, and he is still at Khyentse Rinpoche's monastery. He is one of the monks the scientists have conducted experiments on, so he's certified as a good meditator! The book is simply a joy to read and a perfect one to hand out to friends and family with whom you'd like to begin sharing all this.

In 2010 he followed *Happiness* with a book called *Why Meditate: Working with Thoughts and Emotions, Hay House, Inc.,* 2010, which includes an audio download. I think this could be a very helpful aid for anyone who would actually like to give meditation a go. Again, he's a Vajrayana master, so his would be an excellent preparation for those who like this path. Anything by this author is invaluable.

David R. Loy. *The World Is Made of Stories.* Boston: Wisdom Publications, 2010. In this pithy book, Loy poetically shows us JUST how much our experience is a movie of our own making.

Dacher Keltner, Jason Marsh, and Jeremy Adam Smith. *The Compassionate Instinct.* New York: W. W. Norton, 2010. Through stories and studies, the authors reveal the Buddha Nature in us all, ready to come forth at any time, often at surprising times.

Stephen Post, PhD, and Jill Neimark. *Why Good Things Happen to Good People.* New York: Broadway Books, 2008. This scientifically grounded book is an accessible, enjoyable read. Inspiring. The main study they refer to is a longitudinal study that involves in-depth annual interviews of the subjects over their entire adult lives.

Shantideva. *The Way of the Bodhisattva.* Translated by Padmakara Translation Group. Boston: Shambhala Publications, 2006. This is the all-time classic for advice on how to bring bodhicitta into your life. Lots of helpful, grounded metaphors and reframes.

Sharon Salzberg and Joseph Goldstein. *Insight Meditation: A Step-by-Step Course on How to Meditate.* Boulder, CO: Sounds True, 2001. This is a complete multimedia kit that is the best, most accessible introduction that I know of for Westerners just starting to meditate. I find it helpful too! It's not Vajrayana style, though, so you might want to keep your eyes and mouth open, etc., as I've instructed you in this book. Joseph Goldstein has written other books with the same title, but I thought you might want this kit, put out by Sounds True. Interestingly, both authors are also Dzogchen (Vajrayana) meditators. They have been involved in the Mind and Life group (scientists and the Dalai Lama) for many years.

Sangharakshita. *What Is the Sangha? The Nature of the Spiritual Community.* Cambridge, UK: Windhorse Publications, 2004. Sangharakshita is a Westerner, deeply steeped in Buddhism, who can explain those understandings to the Western mind in a way that we can relate to. He's very much done it for us here with the concept of Jewel of the Sangha—not just as an understanding but as a practice.

Sangharakshita has also written *Who Is the Buddha?* (2008) and *What Is the Dharma?* (2004), so he's covered all Three Jewels!

Just about anything by Pema Chödrön, especially *Start Where You Are.* Boston: Shambhala Publications, 2001. And that same book turned into a beautiful little kit called *The Compassion Box.* This is an ancient course on how to bring bodhicitta into your life and use your life for growing your bodhicitta. It's been popular all these years because it works. Pema Chödrön really tells it like it is, as a modern American, and at the same time is a highly qualified teacher of Vajrayana.

Anam Thubten. *No Self, No Problem.* Point Richmond, CA: Dharmata Press, 2006. This is a great little book written by a true lama, but very accessible to a Westerner. It's pithy and full of gems that guide our minds in the direction we'd like them to go. He teaches Shamata regularly.

Any book by Mingyur Rinpoche. He also teaches Shamata regularly, as do an increasing number of his advanced, highly qualified students. They teach Ngöndro and other practices too. You can check all of this out on his website, www.tergar.org.

Dzigar Kongtrül. *It's Up to You: The Practice of Self-Reflection on the Buddhist Path.* Boston and London: Shambhala Publications, 2006. This is another pithy book, full of helpful thoughts and perspectives, from a genuine lama who also speaks English.

Anything (and there's a lot of it) by B. Alan Wallace. He is highly qualified to speak about Buddhism, science, and Contemplative Science. He was a monk in the Vajrayana lineage, studied under many lamas, and has translated for many of them. He then went on to get a degree in physics. Now he is one of the scholars working with His Holiness the Dalai Lama in developing the new field they call Contemplative Science. He is one of the key people doing the Shamata Project, measuring the brains and bodies of novice meditators as they do three-month intensive Buddhist retreats.

THREE BOOKS BY THUBTEN CHODRON

Buddhism for Beginners. Ithaca, NY: Snow Lion Publications, 2001.

Don't Believe Everything You Think: Living with Wisdom and Compassion. Ithaca, NY: Snow Lion Publications, 2013.

Working With Anger. Ithaca, NY: Snow Lion Publications, 2001.

Thubten Chodron is a Western Buddhist nun who speaks in a very down-to-earth way about the principles of Buddhism. Because she has applied these principles in her own life, she does a beautiful job of helping us apply them in our own.

BRAIN SCIENCE

Richard J. Davidson, PhD, with Sharon Begley. *The Emotional Life of Your Brain: How Its Unique Patterns Affect the Way You Think, Feel, and Live—and How You Can Change Them.* Reprint edition. New York: Plume, 2013. A long subtitle, but truly descriptive. Dr. Davidson is among the top neuroscientists in the growing field of Contemplative Science, which studies the effects of meditation on the brain, with full scientific rigor. He works closely with His Holiness the Dalai Lama. Given Dr. Davidson's accomplishments, we might expect to not be able to understand a thing—so it's a pleasant surprise to discover how readable and accessible this book is. Not one to leave it as an academic study, he has practiced meditation for many years. He is a living poster child of how richly we can cultivate positive habits of mind.

SEVEN POINT MIND TRAINING BOOKS AND MEDIA

If you're wondering what to do with the 23+ hours of the day when you're not on the cushion, I highly recommend you check out Lojong, a.k.a. the Seven Point Mind Training teachings. Why? Because it takes you by the hand and shows you how you can use life's everyday challenges to further your progress. Pema Chödrön offers Lojong materials in a variety of formats: books, audio, cards, etc. She often teaches Lojong, so you could also attend a live teaching. There are probably others who teach it, but I haven't experienced their teachings so I can't speak with authority on them. There are many commentaries on this classic by Chekawa Yeshe Dorje.

We have a short Lojong course on our own website, with recorded teachings containing a few minutes of guided meditations. https://ecourse.namchak .org/courses

Traleg Kyabgon. *The Practice of Lojong: Cultivating Compassion through Training the Mind.* Boston and London: Shambhala Publications, 2007. This book is long but readable and includes some of the relevant neuroscience.

There is video of His Holiness the Dalai Lama giving a teaching on Seven Point Mind Training.

Dilgo Khyentse Rinpoche. *Enlightened Courage.* Translated by Padmakara Translation Group. Ithaca, NY: Snow Lion Publications, 1993 and 2006. Dilgo Khyentse Rinpoche was one of the great scholars and practitioners of the twentieth century. He was the head of the Nyingma Lineage, historically the most populous in Vajrayana. He lived this text to the utmost. He was able to speak its true meaning in down-to-earth terms.

Pema Chödrön. *Start Where You Are.* Boston: Shambhala Publications, 2001. This is the most accessible for Westerners. My one quibble is that she refers to the maxims as "slogans," a term she got from Chögyam Trungpa Rinpoche. If you looked up the definitions of both words, it would be *maxim*, not *slogan*, that would mean "words to live by." A slogan is a phrase you use to sell a car or a political candidate. Oh well, that's a minor point. I still highly recommend this book!

Pema Chödrön also has MP3s of courses and talks she has given on this training.

Pema Chödrön. *The Compassion Box.* Boston and London: Shambhala Publications, 2003.When in doubt, get this one. It includes the book listed above, as well as beautiful cards with a maxim on the front and her explanation on the back. There is a little stand so you can have it on your desk or in your kitchen, reminding you of your theme for the day.

Jamgon Kongtrül. *The Great Path of Awakening: The Classic Guide to Lojong, a Tibetan Buddhist Practice for Cultivating the Heart of Compassion.* Translated by Ken McCleod. Boston and London: Shambhala Publications, 2005. Jamgon Kongtrül "the Great" was among the most influential masters in the nineteenth century in Tibet. This is his commentary, beautifully translated by Ken McCleod. I turn to this one at least as much as any of the others.

Chögyam Trungpa. *Training the Mind and Cultivating Loving-Kindness.* Boston and London: Shambhala Publications,1993. My one quibble with this, again, is the use of *slogan* instead of *maxim*. Though his English was excellent, it wasn't his first language. In the case of this one word choice, perhaps it shows. Since he was Pema Chödrön's Root Lama, it's no wonder she uses the word *slogan*, despite her being American.

FUN & INSPIRING READING

Anna M. Cox. *Just As the Breeze Blows Through Moonlight: The Spiritual Life Journey of Thupten Heruka, a 19th C. Tibetan Yogi.* Bloomington, IN: Xlibris, 2002. This story—both an outer and inner adventure, set in old Tibet—came to Cox after she had been a practitioner for a long time. I didn't want to put it down. I was sad when it was over and I had to leave that world. One of those rare indulgences that's good for you.

Vicki Mackenzie. *Cave In the Snow: Tenzin Palmo's Quest for Enlightenment.* New York: Bloomsbury Publishing, 1998. This is the life story of an Englishwoman who found her way to great Tibetan masters in India, then spent twelve years practicing in a cave in Lhadak. She's come back to tell us about it. Very readable and inspiring.

Ani Tenzin Palmo. *Reflections on a Mountain Lake: Teachings on Practical Buddhism*. Ithaca, NY: Snow Lion Publications, 2002. This is Ani (nun) Tenzin Palmo's own book. It's full of advice and inspiration that's lovely to take in—in sips—and savor.

WEBSITES

Well, of course, there's ours: **Namchak.org** and **NamchakPublishing.com**. We have a lot of free teachings there, including online courses, opportunities to connect with others in your area and beyond, a little Sangha store, and more. You'll recognize some of the contents of this book, and audio or video support for some of its content, including Shamata, Tonglen, and Clearing the Stale Energies. Other articles and teachings come and go too. We also have a large and growing library of print, audio, and visual teachings from our own lamas.

A fun and intriguing one is **spaceandmotion.com**. It combines a lot of different areas of knowledge, including histories of science and various branches of philosophy. My one caveat is that the website includes what I consider some questionable "science." The scientists represented there are respected by many, though considered controversial by some. But then, so was Galileo, in his time. If you liked *The Holographic Universe*, you'll be interested in this website.

Anam Thubten's website: **dharmata.org**.

Mingyur Rinpoche's website: **tergar.org**.

The Mind and Life group's website (**mindandlife.org**) offers a lot of historical and current thought on cosmology, with the goal of seeing how current scientific thought on the subject fits with Buddhist cosmology.

Dr. Richard J. Davidson's website: **centerhealthyminds.org**. This is one of my favorite brain science websites. They are doing cutting-edge research on such fascinating topics as the measurable effects of meditation on DNA, classroom behavior improvement through meditation, and measurably positive effects on military veterans who practice meditation.

Appendix D: Credits & Permissions

This page is a continuation of the copyright page. Grateful acknowledgment is made for permission granted to reproduce images and to use quotes in the text.

PHOTOS & IMAGES

Pages: iii, iv, x, xii, xiv, xvii, xviii, xxii, 20–21, 62, 63, 76, 78, 87, 88, 105, 107, 109, 110, 115, 116, 120, 129, 130, 134, 135, 136, bookmark and practice cards: From *The Encyclopedia of Tibetan Symbols and Motifs* by Robert Beer, © 1999 by Robert Beer. Reprinted by arrangement with Shambhala Publications, Inc., Boulder, CO. www. shambhala.com

Page ix: © 2019 Namchak Publishing Company LLC, photo by Erika Peterman

Page xi, xxii–xxiii, 1: © 2017 Namchak LLC, photo courtesy of Keegan Connell

Page xii, xvi: © 2014 Lama Tsomo LLC

Page xiv: Brenda Ahearn photo. © 2010 Daily Inter Lake. Reprinted with permission of Daily Inter Lake. No unauthorized use permitted.

Pages xx–xxi, 4, 8–9, 10, 28: Photos © 2006 Alison Wright; page xix: Photo © 2007 Alison Wright; page 106: Photo © 2009 Alison Wright; page xxiv: Photo © 2010 Alison Wright; page 64: Photo © 2011 Alison Wright

Pages 2, 35, 42–43, 68, 75, 82–83, 131: Photos © 2012 Radd Icenoggle.

Pages 11, 14 (3), 15 (2), 16 (3), 17 (3), 19 (3), 33: Photos © 2014 Lama Tsomo LLC; Photos by Crackle Photography

Pages 22–23: Rita Januskeviciute/Shutterstock.com

Page 29: Photo by Eskay Lim. Depositphotos.com

Page 36: Photo by YAYImages. Depositphotos.com

Page 48: Jeanie333/Shutterstock.com

Page 53: Photo by Hamza Nouasria on Unsplash

Pages 56–57: Photo of Arrol Oxford. © 2014 Mercedes Oxford; used by permission. Unauthorized reproduction prohibited

Page 60: Jason Stitt/Shutterstock.com

Page 65: George Marcel/Shutterstock.com

Pages 86, 89: Photos © 2014 Lama Tsomo LLC

Page 93: Brett Jorgensen/Shutterstock.com

Practice cards: Refuge Visualization (Vajradhara and Mandharava): Image courtesy of Namchak LLC; White Tara: Image courtesy of Lama Tsomo LLC; Clearing the Stale Energies: Photos © 2014 Lama Tsomo LLC; Photos by Crackle Photography

QUOTES

Page 18: Excerpt from "Every Foot a Shrine," from *Love Poems from God: Twelve Sacred Voices from the East and West* by Daniel Ladinsky, © 2002, and used with permission.

Pages 20–21, 37: *The Mindful Brain: Reflection and Attunement in the Cultivation of Well-Being* by Daniel Siegel. Publisher: W. W. Norton & Company. © 2007 Mind Your Brain, Inc.

Page 29: *The Principles of Psychology, Vol. 1*, by William James, Dover Publications; Revised ed. edition (June 1, 1950), published by special arrangement with Henry Holt and Company. © 1890 Henry Holt & Co.

Page 49: Brief excerpt from p. 77 from *Don't Just Do Something, Sit There: A Mindfulness Retreat* by Sylvia Boorstein. Copyright © 1996 by Sylvia Boorstein. Reprinted by permission of HarperCollins Publishers.

Page 85: Elizabeth Mattis-Namgyel, quoted in the article "Pema Chödrön on 4 Keys to Waking Up," by Andrea Miller. © March 2014 issue of *Shambhala Sun*.

Practice Card Dedication/Aspiration prayer courtesy of Yongey Mingyur Rinpoche and the Tergar Meditation Community.

Index

Lama Sangak Yeshe Tsomo

CURRICULUM VITAE

Education & Professional Training

2006–present: One to two months' retreat annually, with instruction and guidance from Tulku Sangak Rinpoche and Khen Rinpoche.

1995–present: Scores of teachings, empowerments, and pilgrimages, including the following:

- One-week and two-week Dark retreat instruction retreats with Tulku Sangak Rinpoche and Khen Rinpoche (2017–present).
- Semiannual ten-day Dzogchen instruction retreats with Tulku Sangak Rinpoche (2006–2010).
- Six years of ten-day instruction retreats on *The Treasury of Precious Qualities*, a classic text that includes the entire Buddhist path. Tulku Sangak Rinpoche, Khen Rinpoche, and Anam Thubten Rinpoche, instructors.
- Finished Ngöndro (Preliminary Practices). This involved 108,000 prostrations; 108,000 repetitions of the 100-Syllable Mantra; 1,200,000 recitations of the Vajra Guru Mantra; and other similarly extensive practices.
- Small-group meeting with His Holiness the Dalai Lama. Ann Arbor, Michigan (April 2008).
- Tenshuk offering to His Holiness the Dalai Lama. Dharamsala, India (as part of a ten-day pilgrimage, July 2007).
- Two interviews with His Holiness the Dalai Lama.

2005 in Nepal and 2006 in the US: Lama ordination (bestowed by Tulku Sangak Rinpoche).

1995–2005: Ongoing intensive lama training in the Nyingma tradition, with Rinpoche. The following were among the components of the training:

- Thirty 1- to 2-week training intensives.
- Traditional three-year retreat, in strict, solitary retreat conditions, under Rinpoche's direct supervision, progressing from one stage of training to the next, finishing with the highest levels of Dzogchen practice. The practice retreats were usually done three months at a time.
- Several months of study and training at Rinpoche's monastery in Nepal.
- Ongoing scholarly and spiritual study of numerous classic Vajrayana Buddhist texts.
- Increased responsibility as a teacher under Rinpoche's guidance.
- Learned to speak fluent Tibetan, allowing ability to chant in Tibetan while understanding the meaning, to act as translator for students and practitioners, and perhaps most important, to speak extensively with Rinpoche and Khen Rinpoche, as well as other lamas, about the Dharma.

1990: MA, Counseling Psychology, Antioch University (emphasis: Jungian
studies).

1987: BA, Counseling Psychology, Antioch University.

Affiliations & Memberships

Namchak Foundation, Montana. Co-founder, current board member.

Academy for the Love of Learning, Santa Fe, New Mexico. Founding Board
member.

Ewam (US and international nonprofit center and school). Founding board
member, board member, 1999–2004.

Light of Berotsana translation group, Boulder, Colorado. Board member,
2002–2008.

Namchak Foundation (US and international group with physical and online
presence, dedicated to supporting people of the Namchak Lineage in Tibet
and developing retreat sites). Co-founder with Namchak Dorlop Dorje
Lopön Choeji Lodoe.

Pleasant Ridge Waldorf School, Viroqua, Wisconsin. Founder and board
member, ca. 1975.

Selected Publications

The Dharma of Dogs: Our Best Friends as Spiritual Teachers, edited by Tami Simon.
Sounds True, 2017. "Lama Kusung," pp. 33–35.

Why Is the Dalai Lama Always Smiling? (the earlier incarnation of this book and
Book 2: *Wisdom & Compassion*). Namchak Publishing, 2016.

*The Lotus & The Rose: Conversations Between Tibetan Buddhism and Mystical
Christianity, with the Reverend Dr. Matthew Fox.* Namchak Publishing, 2018.

"Ani Tsering Wangmo: A Life of Merit" in *Lion's Roar Newsletter*, March 2010.

"Coming Home" in *Originally Blessed*. Creation Spirituality Communities, 2008.

"Dharmasala" in *Lion's Roar Newsletter*, August 2007.

"Shedra" in *Lion's Roar Newsletter*, February 2006.

Selected Presentations & Teachings

"Expanding Capacities for Joy and Connection: Science and Practice," plenary
session with Richard Davidson, PhD, and Lama Tsomo, Greater Good
Science Center "Science of Happiness" Conference.

A variety of teachings, including weekly and short retreats (2005–present)
when on-site at the Ewam center and at other US and international sites,
including the New School in New York, Spirit Rock in California, East Bay
Meditation Center, etc.

"Building the 'We' Economy from the Inside Out," COCAP 2019. Solo talk on
compassion, then plenary session with Angel Kyodo Williams, Reverend
Deborah Johnson, Konda Mason, and others.

Book launch events for *The Lotus and The Rose*, including "An Evening with
Lama Tsomo and Matthew Fox," Sacred Stream, Berkeley, California; "East
Meets West at Grace Cathedral," San Francisco.

Book launch events for *Why Is the Dalai Lama Always Smiling?* including "A Conversation with Van Jones," New York City; "A Conversation with Lama Tsomo and Sharon Salzberg," New York City; "Google Talks with Lama Tsomo," Mountain View, California.

Multiple co-presentations, including weekend retreats/workshops with Aaron Stern, founder of the Academy for the Love of Learning, and with Khen Rinpoche.

Three-hour introduction to Tibetan Buddhism, shown on TV in Taiwan. This was posted on YouTube in five installments.

Two guest appearances at the University of Montana School of Social Work. 2011.

"Once Existing from Self, Your Life Target Will Come Out Like Art Creation" (presentation to educators, students, artists, and general public). Miaolie Pottery. Miaolie, Taiwan. May 2010.

"Solving Confusion in the Mind" (presentation to Taiwan Sunshine Women's Association). Taichung Ewam Centre. Taichung, Taiwan. May 2010.

"Experience Sharing: To Change Your Life and Career from Miserable to Successful by Learning the Methods of Mind Observation Training" (talk to twenty-five business owners and senior managers). Howard Hotel. Taipei, Taiwan. April 2010.

"Learning Buddhism" retreat. Taichung Ewam Centre. Taichung, Taiwan. April 2010.

"Learning Buddhism and Doing Practices to Clarify Confusion." Howard Hotel. Taipei, Taiwan. April 2010.

"Seven Point Mind Training." Yung Ho Training Centre. Taiwan. March 2010.

"Seven Point Mind Training, 3rd Installment," retreat. Ewam. Arlee, Montana. November 2009.

"Inner Peace/Outer Peace: What Is the Relationship?" (with Frances Moore Lappé). Peace Festival. Ewam. Arlee, Montana. September 2009.

"Seven Point Mind Training, 2nd Installment," retreat. Ewam. Arlee, Montana. May 2009.

"Seven Point Mind Training, 1st Installment," retreat. Ewam. Arlee, Montana. April 2009.

"Organic Food and Buddhism" (presentation to second-level Buddhists). Howard Hotel. Taipei, Taiwan. March 2009.

"Enjoy Your Life with Happiness" and "From Common Happiness to Common Bodhi." Taipei Shilin Resort. Taipei, Taiwan. March 2009.

"Gratitude; Visualization; Dreams Come True, as Your Wishes." National Normal University. Taipei, Taiwan. March 2009.

Ngöndro retreat. Ewam Center. Hong Kong. November 2008.

"Buddhism." Unitarian Universalist Church. Missoula, Montana. May 2008.

"How to Make Your Mind Happy" (seminar). National Normal University. Taipei, Taiwan. March 2008.

"Keep Your Soul and Spirit in Good Health—Removing Torments and Mastering Your Spirit." Taichung County Cultural Center. Taichung, Taiwan. March 2008.

"Skillful Means Using Dharma to Benefit Others in Our Daily Lives." Ewam Center. Hong Kong. March 2008.

"Interaction and Modification of the Buddha Dharma Internal Spirit." Haufan University. Taipei, Taiwan. March 2008.

"Transforming Inner and Outer Worlds: Christian Mysticism and Tibetan Buddhism" (presentation with the Reverend Dr. Matthew Fox). Jung Center of Houston. February 2008.

"East Meets West: Christian Mysticism and Tibetan Buddhism" (presentation with the Reverend Dr. Matthew Fox). Stanford University Continuing Studies. Palo Alto, California. June 2007.

"Skills to Face Suffering" (Tonglen or Tranquil Abiding presentation to cancer patients). Tuen Mun Hospital. Hong Kong. January 2007.

"A Journey to a Peaceful Mind" (presentation to social workers and clients). City Hall Conference Room. Hong Kong. January 2007.

"How to Handle Suffering" (presentation to nursing staff). Tuen Mun Hospital. Hong Kong. January 2007.

"The Lotus and the Cross/The Lotus and the Rose" (invitation-only dialogue with the Reverend Dr. Matthew Fox). Academy for the Love of Learning. Location: Upaya Zen Center. Santa Fe, New Mexico. November 2006.

Series of interviews and presentations on Life TV, Taiwan (a 24-hour nationwide TV station devoted to Buddhist teachings). Topics included "The Pursuit of Happiness" (part of Woman Psychology Seminars). December 2006.

"Introduction to Buddhism and Buddhist Practice" (thirty-hour intensive course). University of Creation Spirituality. San Francisco, California. 2005.

Buddhist retreat (leader) on Ngöndro. Academy for the Love of Learning. Santa Fe, New Mexico. Location: Upaya Zen Center. Santa Fe, New Mexico. May 2005.

Tulku Sangak Rinpoche consecrating the stupas at the Namchak Retreat Ranch

Acknowledgments

It seems only right to begin with my family. My parents permanently infected me with the joy of exploring the nature of reality and understanding people. During my growing-up years, my sister sat with me for hours as we passionately replicated that pursuit. She's the real writer in the family, not to mention a brilliant editor, and she's always graciously encouraged my efforts.

I also want to thank Herman Schaalman, my family's rabbi, who gave me my first guidance and pointed me in the right direction in my pursuit of wisdom.

Four more whom I wish to acknowledge are my dogs Gonpo, Soongma, Kusung, and Dawa, my loving companions over the many years of writing this book . . . well, except for one writing stint at the monastery in Nepal. I deeply regretted that they were too big to fit in my carry-on bag.

I'm a teacher, and this series is a succession of many teachings. If it weren't for all of the students over the years and decades, I would not know what or how to teach. If it weren't for students' needs calling this forth from me, I wouldn't have troubled myself to write it. If it weren't for future students, I certainly wouldn't have written it. For all of this, and such inspiring open-mindedness and open-heartedness, I'm deeply grateful.

I feel a great deal of gratitude for my editor, Michael Frisbie, who is not only top-notch at the art of editing, but a natural and accomplished educator. Given that this was my first real attempt at a full-length book, I needed both of those gifts in great measure. Had it not been for him, this book would have been just a nice manual. That is what I'd originally had in mind. But because of his genuine enthusiasm for the material (despite not being a Buddhist) and his skills, his questions and comments evoked the rest of this book, which was actually in there somewhere. He always gave generously, and with good humor. Actually a hysterical sense of humor!

Huge thanks to Mary Ann Casler for her lovely work on the design, layout, and images for the original version of this book, which was titled *Why Is the Dalai Lama Always Smiling?* She guided us expertly through the galley and print process, as well as myriad details involved in publishing a book. For the beautiful layout and design of this new volume, applause to Kate Basart, who is not only skillful but a pleasure to work with. Thanks to Erin Cusick for her care and skill in proofreading, and to Colleen Kane from Namchak Publishing, for holding the many threads that wove together for the final product. Many thanks to Merry Sun for her excellent editing with a Millennial take; I would have no idea!

Much gratitude to the entire Namchak team, who contributed to the many aspects of putting a book together and sending it off into the world. I'm especially thinking of Keegan in IT, for wrestling Word to the ground repeatedly, and to Mitch, for jumping in as needed. Much gratitude to Jessica Larson, director of Education and Outreach, for her many key roles in bringing this out into the world. A few people supported in their consulting roles, with great skill and genuine enthusiasm: Jenny Best, Liz Koch, and especially Anne Tillery, founder of Pyramid Communications.

Many thanks to Janna Glasser, not only for her excellent tracking down of the shocking number of permissions for this book, but for the various legal agreements as well. But beyond that she is one of our more ardent supporters. Thanks to Jason Hicks, aided and abetted by Deborah Hicks, for recording the audio version of this entire book—no small feat! Gratitude to JoAnn Hogan for managing the countless details necessary for the success of this project.

Arthur Zajonc, emeritus professor of physics at Amherst and past president of Mind and Life Institute, was kind enough to read and comment on the physics tidbits. Dr. Richard Davidson, one of the neuroscientists in the Mind and Life Institute working with His Holiness the Dalai Lama xiv, and head of the Center for Healthy Minds and of the Waisman Center at the University of Wisconsin–Madison, took precious time from his busy schedule to talk to me and review my neuroscience pieces.

Lama Chönam and Sangye Khandro, co-founders of the Light of Berotsana translation group, read an early version of my manuscript and gave me lots of crucial feedback, corrections, and encouragement. Tulku (title meaning "reincarnated abbot") Anam Thubten Rinpoche, from whom I've been fortunate enough to receive teachings, read and gave me helpful comments and great encouragement on my nearly finished manuscript. Also in the Experts on Tibetan Buddhism camp was Namchak Dorlop (full name Namchak Dorje Lopön Choeji Lodoe), Tulku Sangak Rinpoche's brother, who reviewed the manuscript for accuracy.

As always, I'm deeply grateful for my co-conspirator in many things, beloved/adopted kin, and "witness to my life," Aaron Stern.

I feel these acknowledgments must include—and highlight—the masters of the Namchak Lineage, our particular branch of the larger Nyingma Lineage, beginning with Guru Rinpoche and Nup Sangye Yeshe, who hid the teachings, then Tsasum Lingpa, who later revealed those teachings, continuing in an unbroken thread of wisdom, down to the present world lineage holder, Tulku Sangak Rinpoche, to whom this book is dedicated. And my deep gratitude to Namchak Khen Rinpoche, Tulku Sangak Rinpoche's brother, who has also taught me much Dharma. Perhaps his greatest teaching is his living evidence of its efficacy. The most recent revealer of the teachings of our lineage was Pedgyal Lingpa, who passed them directly to Tulku Sangak Rinpoche. Without every one of the lineage lamas passing the wisdom down from one to the next with utmost care, I would not have received the gems that I talk about in this book. A lineage of teachings that is revealed and passed down in this way is referred to as a treasure. And that's actually an understatement.

I wouldn't want to receive all that Rinpoche and those who came before have offered me and not transmit what I can. Whenever I felt my lack of readiness too keenly, I also had this thought: if I had come upon this book when I was much younger, I know that I would have been delighted to use it as a beginning. If this book turns out to be of benefit to you, then my purpose for writing it will have been fulfilled.

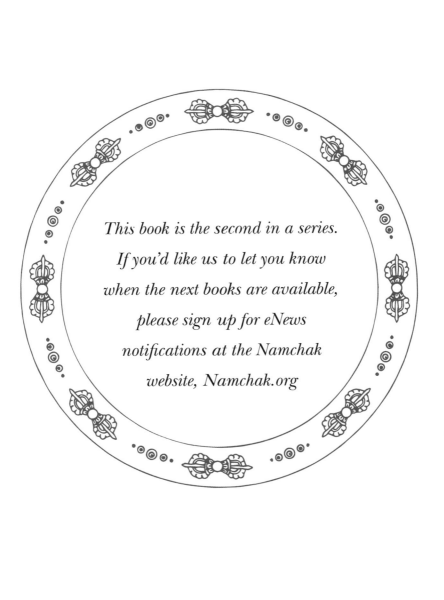

This book is the second in a series.
If you'd like us to let you know
when the next books are available,
please sign up for eNews
notifications at the Namchak
website, Namchak.org